MICROSOFT WORKS
in easy steps

Stephen Copestake

COMPUTER
STEP

In easy steps is an imprint of Computer Step
Southfield Road . Southam
Warwickshire CV33 OFB . England

Tel: 01926 817999 Fax: 01926 817005
http://www.computerstep.com

Second edition, 1998

Notice of Liability

Every effort has been made to ensure that this book contains accurate
and current information. However, Computer Step and the author shall
not be liable for any loss or damage suffered by readers as a result of
any information contained herein.

Trademarks

Microsoft® and Windows® are registered trademarks of Microsoft
Corporation. All other trademarks are acknowledged as belonging to
their respective companies.

Printed and bound in the United Kingdom

ISBN 1-84078-001-0

Contents

3 The Spreadsheet 101

4 The Database 149

Index 189

A Common Approach

This chapter shows you how Works provides a common look, so you can get started quickly in any module. You'll learn how to create new documents and open/save existing ones. You'll also learn how to how to use Note-It (the inbuilt Works notation utility) and create/edit address books. Finally, you'll get information you need from Works' on-line HELP system.

Covers

Introduction

Microsoft Works consists of three principal modules:

- The Word Processor
- The Spreadsheet
- The Database

In a sense, these are 'cut-down' versions of Microsoft Word, Excel and Access. In spite of this, however, all three modules provide a high level of functionality and ease of use.

Another great advantage of Works is that it integrates the three modules exceptionally well. They share a common look and feel.

The illustration below shows the Word Processor opening screen. Flagged are components which are common to the other modules, too.

 Works also provides a further module: Communications. However, this isn't covered within this book. Any reference to 'Works modules' therefore refers solely to the Word Processor, Spreadsheet and Database.

 Although the Toolbar appears in each Works module, the contents vary somewhat from module to module.

 For how to use and customise the Toolbar, see later in this Chapter.

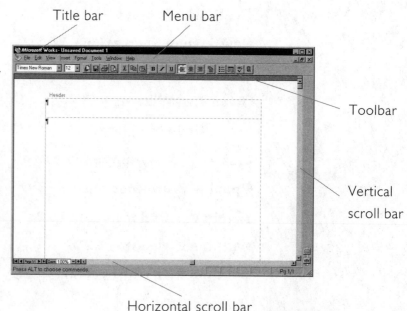

Title bar   Menu bar

Toolbar

Vertical scroll bar

Horizontal scroll bar

...contd

Compare the Word Processor screen on page 8 with the following:

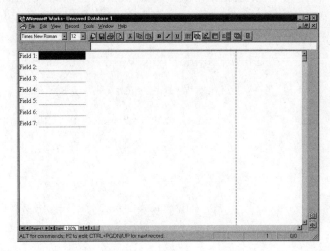

Database screen

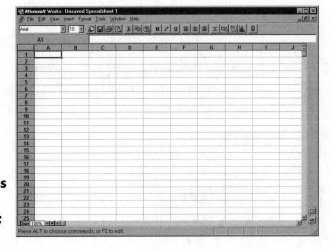

Spreadsheet screen

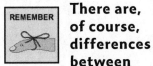

There are, of course, differences between the module screens; we'll explore these in later chapters.

Notice that many of the screen components are held in common. The purpose of this shared approach is to ensure that users of Works can move between modules with the minimum of re-adjustment.

The Works Toolbar

The Toolbar is an important component in all three Works modules. A toolbar is an on-screen bar which contains shortcut buttons. These symbolise (and allow easy access to) often used commands which would normally have to be invoked via one or more menus.

For example, The Word Processor's toolbar lets you:

- launch other modules

- create, open, save and print documents

- perform copy and paste and cut and paste operations

- align text

- embolden, italicise or underline text

- apply a new typeface and/or type size to text

- spell-check text

by simply clicking on the relevant button.

The Toolbar varies to some extent from module to module.

Hiding/revealing the Toolbar

In the Word Processor, Spreadsheet or Database, pull down the View menu. Do the following:

 **The ✔ signifies that the Toolbar is currently visible.**

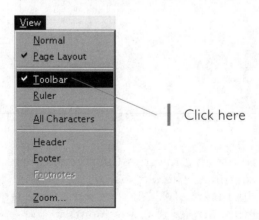

Click here

Adding buttons to the Toolbar

By default, the pre-defined Toolbar which appears in the Works modules has only a small number of buttons associated with it. For instance, the Word Processor version has 18. However, just about all editing operations you can perform from within Works menus can be incorporated as a button within the Toolbar, for ease of access.

To do this, first make sure the Toolbar is visible on-screen (see earlier for how to do this). Pull down the Tools menu and click Customize Toolbar. Now do the following:

Click the menu to which you want the button added

Repeat steps 2 to 4 as often as necessary.

If in doubt, left-click any button in the dialog and hold down the mouse button; Works tells you what the selected button does in the Description field.

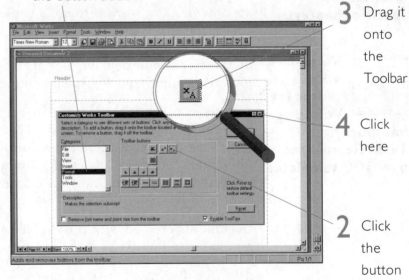

3 Drag it onto the Toolbar

4 Click here

2 Click the button

Removing buttons from the Toolbar

If you no longer want a button to appear on the Toolbar, pull down the Tools menu and click Customize Toolbar. When the Customize Works Toolbar dialog has launched (see above), click the relevant button. Drag it off the Toolbar. Then follow step 4 above.

New document creation

All Works modules let you:

- create new blank documents

- create new documents with the help of a 'TaskWizard'

- create new documents based on a 'template' you've created yourself, or (in the case of version 4.5) on pre-supplied, professionals templates

Because the Word Processor, Database and Spreadsheet modules are uniform in the way they create new documents, we'll look at this topic here rather than in later module-specific chapters.

Creating blank documents is the simplest route to new document creation; use this if you want to define the document components yourself from scratch. This is often not the most efficient way to create new documents.

TaskWizards are a shortcut to the creation of new documents. You work through a series of dialogs, answering the appropriate questions and making the relevant choices. TaskWizards greatly simplify and speed up the creation of new documents while at the same time producing highly professional results.

Version 4.5 of Works for Windows has more TaskWizards, and over 100 templates.

Templates are sample documents complete with the relevant formatting and/or text. They differ from TaskWizards in that there is no question-and-answer interaction. However, by basing a new document on a template, you automatically have access to any inherent text and/or formatting.

Documents created with the use of TaskWizards or templates can easily be amended subsequently.

All three document creation methods involve launching the Works Task Launcher. This is a useful composite dialog which you can also use to open existing Works documents

For more information on opening Works documents, see page 20.

Creating blank documents

You can create a new blank document from within any of the Works modules.

The first step is to launch the Task Launcher. From within the relevant module, pull down the File menu and click New. Now do the following:

You can use a keyboard shortcut to run the Task Launcher. Simply press Ctrl+N.

Ensure this tab is active

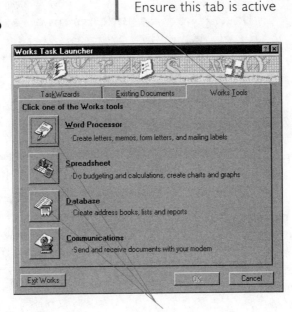

If you're creating a new database, Works doesn't immediately comply; before it can do so, you need to define the necessary fields. See Chapter 4 for how to do this.

2 Click the relevant module

Running the Task Launcher automatically

If you want to create a new blank document immediately after you've started Works, you don't need to launch the Task Launcher manually: it appears automatically.

Once the Task Launcher is on-screen, however, you can follow the above steps to produce the relevant blank document.

Using TaskWizards

REMEMBER

Version 4.5 of Works has an increased number of TaskWizards: 39, to be precise.

Works provides a large number of TaskWizards, organised under overall category headings. With these, you can create a very wide variety of professional-quality documents. For example, you can create newsletters, CVs, letterheads, memos, brochures, bids, labels, quotations, fax sheets, employee profiles, invoices, phone lists, certificates, theses, school reports, tests . . .

Basing new documents on a TaskWizard

In any of the three principal Works modules, pull down the File menu and click New. The Task Launcher appears. Carry out the following steps:

REMEMBER

For how to use the Address Book TaskWizard, see pages 26-30.

Ensure this tab is active

REMEMBER

The section on the right of the Task Launcher provides a potted description of the selected TaskWizard.

2 Click an overall category

Works Task Launcher

TaskWizards | Existing Documents | Works Tools

Click the TaskWizard you want to begin

Common Tasks
- Address Book
- Letter
- Letterhead
- Newsletter
- Resume (CV)
- Start from Scratch
- **Correspondence**
- **Envelopes and Labels**
- **Business Management**
- **Names and Addresses**
- **Household Management**

Choose a chronological, qualifications, or CV format, and the professionally designed layouts will ensure an attractive appearance for your resume.

List categories in different order

Exit Works | OK | Cancel

3 Click a specific TaskWizard

4 Click here

Works now launches a series of question-and-answer dialogs.

...contd

When you've selected the TaskWizard you want to use, Works launches a series of dialogs which vary accordingly. However, the basic format is the same. Works is asking you to supply it with the minimal information required.

The illustration below is the first stage in most or all TaskWizards. Perform the action indicated.

5 Click here

Now carry out steps 6-7 below:

 The equivalent dialog in other TaskWizards may be slightly different.

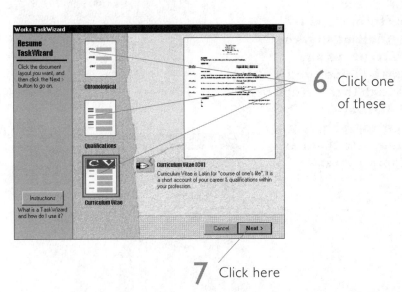

6 Click one of these

7 Click here

...contd

Carry out the following additional steps:

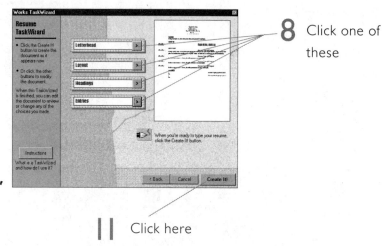

8 Click one of these

11 Click here

REMEMBER

Sometimes, fewer dialogs appear in TaskWizards. For example, if you run the Newsletter TaskWizard, you only need to perform steps 1-7. Additionally, the contents of any extra dialogs you launch (here, steps 9-10) vary considerably; complete them as appropriate.

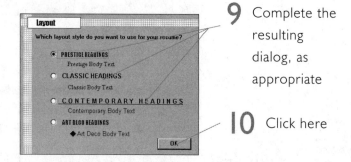

9 Complete the resulting dialog, as appropriate

10 Click here

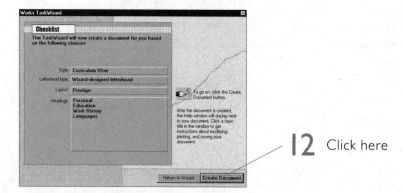

12 Click here

Pre-defined templates New in version 4.5

Works provides a large number of templates, organised under a single overall heading. With these, you can create a very wide variety of professional-quality documents. For example, you can create:

Version 4.5 of Works has over 100 pre-defined templates.

— gift lists

— personal budgets

— conversion tables

— gardening almanacs

— fitness training logs

— moving planners

— menus, recipes and shopping lists

Templates contain pre-defined text and formatting, just like TaskWizards.

— to-do lists

— certificates

— party planners . . .

Templates lack the question-and-answer component of TaskWizards. However, they are quicker to use (and just as effective).

Basing new documents on a template

In any of the Works modules, pull down the File menu and do the following:

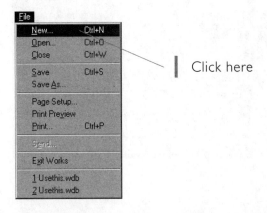
Click here

Now carry out the following additional steps:

2 Ensure this tab is active

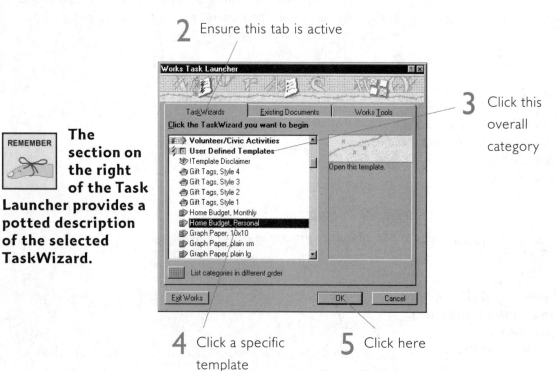

3 Click this overall category

REMEMBER The section on the right of the Task Launcher provides a potted description of the selected TaskWizard.

Open this template.

4 Click a specific template

5 Click here

Works now launches the selected template:

REMEMBER When you've opened the selected template, amend the content and/or formatting, as appropriate.

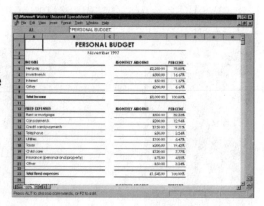

This is a Works spreadsheet, set up as a budget

Creating your own templates

To use a template you've created, follow the procedures on pages 17-18.

In any Works module, you can save an existing document (complete with all text and formatting) as a template. You can then use this template as the basis for new document creation. The text/formatting is immediately carried across.

Saving your work as a template

First, open the document you want to save as a template (for how to do this, see the 'Opening Works documents' topic later). Pull down the File menu and click Save As. Now do the following:

1 Click here. In the drop-down list, click the drive you want to host the template

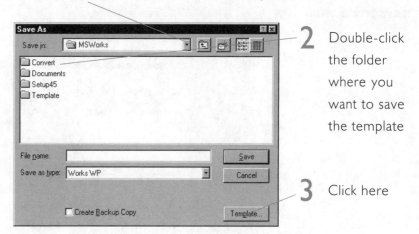

2 Double-click the folder where you want to save the template

3 Click here

5 Click here

4 Type in a name for the new template

Opening Works documents

We saw earlier that Works lets you create new documents in various ways. You can also open Word Processor, Spreadsheet and Database documents you've already created:

HANDY TIP **You can also use the Documents** section of the Windows Startup menu to open recently used Works files – see your Windows documentation for how to do this.

- just after you've started Works

- from within the relevant Works module

Opening an existing document at startup
Immediately after you've started Works, carry out steps 1 and 2, OR 1 and 3, as appropriate:

Ensure this tab is active

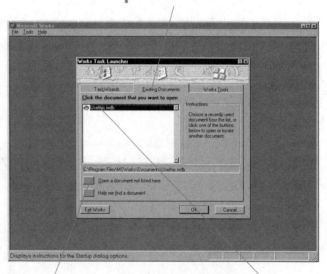

3 Click here if the existing file you need isn't shown in step 2

2 Double-click a recently used file to open it

If you follow steps 1 and 3, the Open dialog appears. See page 21 for how to complete this.

...contd

You can use a keyboard shortcut to launch the Open dialog: simply press Ctrl+O.

HANDY TIP

You can open documents created in formats native to other programs into any Works module (this is called 'importing'). For example, you can import Word for Windows files (but note that features which aren't found in Works are ignored).
  In step 1, select the external format. Then follow steps 2-5.

HANDY TIP

Opening a document from within a module

From within any Works module, pull down the File menu and click Open. Now carry out the following steps, as appropriate:

2 Click here. In the drop-down list, click the drive which hosts the file

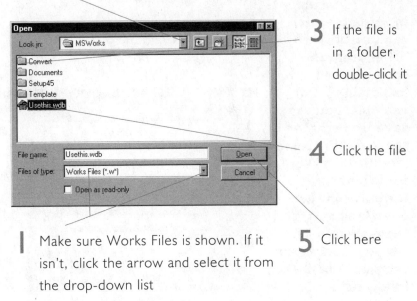

3 If the file is in a folder, double-click it

4 Click the file

1 Make sure Works Files is shown. If it isn't, click the arrow and select it from the drop-down list

5 Click here

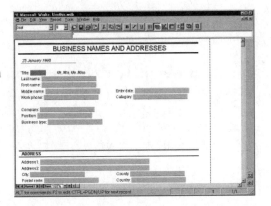

The opened Database file

Saving Works documents

It's important to save your work at frequent intervals, in order to avoid data loss in the event of a hardware fault or power interruption. Works uses a consistent approach to saving throughout its modules.

You can save Works documents in formats which can be utilised by other programs (this is called 'exporting'). For example, you can save files created in the Word Processor module into Word for Windows format, and then open (and edit) them there.

In step 1, select the external format. Then follow steps 2-5.

Saving a document for the first time

In the Word Processor, Spreadsheet or Database modules, pull down the File menu and click Save. Or press Ctrl+S. Now do the following:

2 Click here. In the drop-down list, click the drive you want to host the document

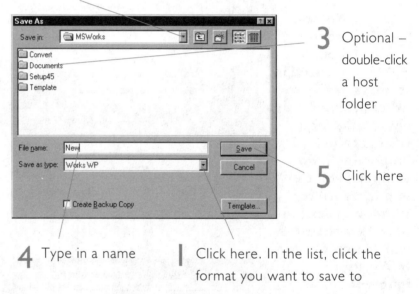

3 Optional – double-click a host folder

5 Click here

4 Type in a name

1 Click here. In the list, click the format you want to save to

Saving previously saved documents

In any of the modules, pull down the File menu and click Save. Or press Ctrl+S. No dialog launches; instead, Works saves the latest version of your document to disk, overwriting the previous version.

Creating notes

You can use a feature called Note-It to insert notes in Word Processor, Spreadsheet or Database documents. Notes consist of text, together with a picture which serves as a marker. The picture is also used to display the associated text. Additionally, notes can have explanatory captions.

To add a note to a database, you must be in Form Design View (see Chapter 4 for more information).

Creating a note

Open the document to which you want to add the note. Position the insertion point at the location where you want the note to appear. Pull down the Insert menu and click Note-It. Now do the following:

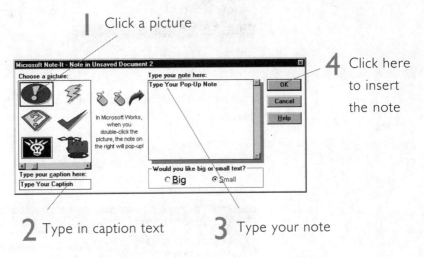

1 Click a picture

4 Click here to insert the note

2 Type in caption text

3 Type your note

The illustration below shows a database with an inserted note:

Note that picture markers within documents can be moved and resized in the normal way.

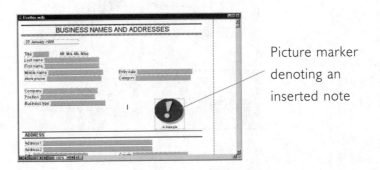

Picture marker denoting an inserted note

Viewing notes

Another way to view an inserted note is simply to double-click it.

Viewing inserted notes

First, click the note to select it. Then pull down the Edit menu and do the following:

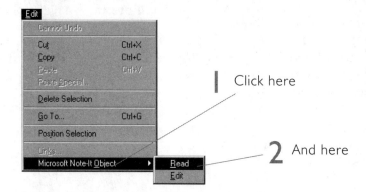

Click here

2 And here

The next illustration shows a note displayed over a database:

Magnified view of note

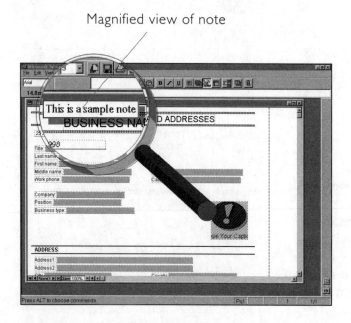

Editing notes

To amend the content of an existing note, click it. Pull down the Edit menu and do the following:

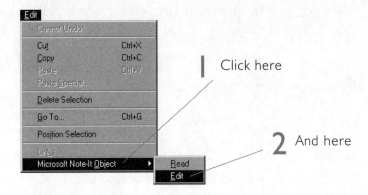

Now carry out step 3 below to assign a new picture to the note, step 4 to amend the caption and/or step 5 to alter the substance of the note text. Finally, carry out step 6 to update the note:

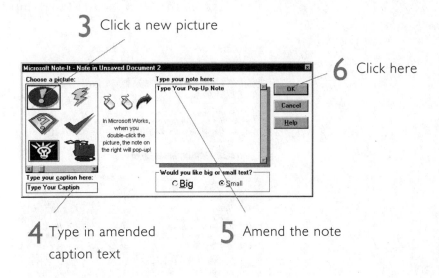

Creating address books

One specific TaskWizard deserves special mention. You can use the Address Book TaskWizard to produce a useful contact database. Once you've done this, you can call it up from within any Works module, with one or two mouse clicks.

You can choose from the following address books:

- Personal

- Business

- Customers or Clients

- Suppliers and Vendors

- Sales Contacts

- Employees

Creating an address book

In any module, pull down the File menu and click New. The Task Launcher appears. Carry out the following steps:

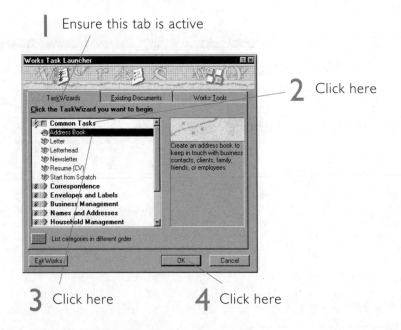

Perform the following additional steps:

5 Click here

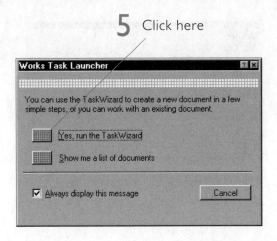

6 Click an address book type

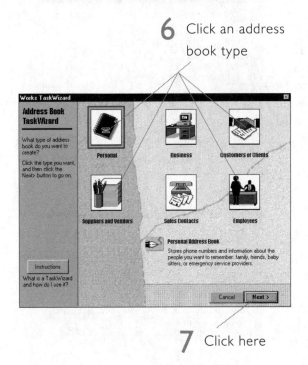

7 Click here

...contd

Perform the following additional steps:

Here, Works summarises the details of the address book, so far.

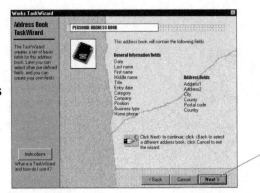

8 Click here

Follow step 9 if you want to amend the address book defaults (e.g. to add additional fields).

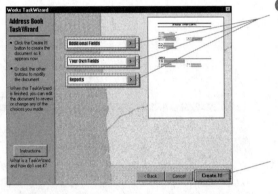

9 Click one or more arrows (then complete the resulting dialog)

10 Click here

Click here: to make this your default address book (see page 29).

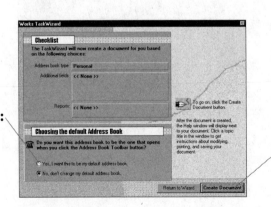

11 Click here to create the address book

Accessing address books

You can:

1. specify a default address book (i.e. one which Works opens automatically when you issue a given command – see below)

2. view the default address book at will, from within any module

Specifying a default address book

Pull down the Tools menu and do the following:

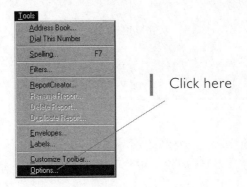

Click here

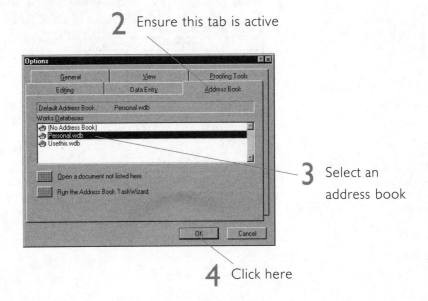

2 Ensure this tab is active

3 Select an address book

4 Click here

Viewing the default address book

From within any module, pull down the Tools menu and do the following:

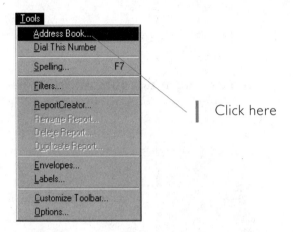

Click here

In the illustration below, Works is displaying the address book database chosen in steps 1-4 on page 29:

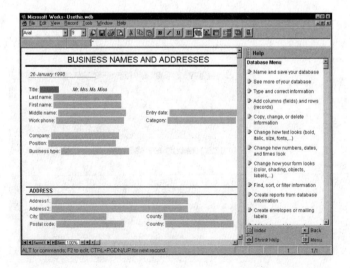

Using HELP Contents

Works has comprehensive Help facilities, organised under two broad headings:

• Contents (a list of topics organised by module)

• Index (an alphabetical list of topics)

You can use a keyboard shortcut to launch Help: simply press F1.

Click the Index or Contents tabs, as appropriate, and then follow the relevant steps.

To generate the Help Contents dialog from within any module, pull down the Help menu and choose Contents.

Using Contents
Do the following:

Click the relevant module

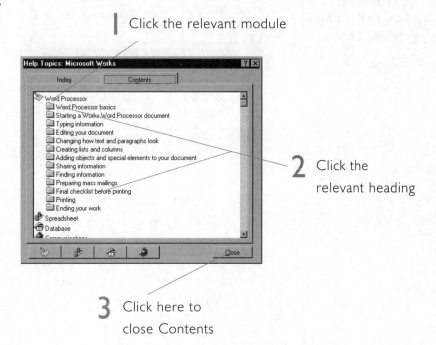

2 Click the relevant heading

3 Click here to close Contents

After step 2, Works launches a series of sub-headings. When you find the topic you want information on (prefixed by 🖹 instead of 📁), click it. (For what happens after step 2, see page 33.)

Finally, carry out step 3.

Using HELP Index

To generate the Help Index dialog, pull down the Help menu and choose Index.

You can use a keyboard shortcut to launch Help: simply press F1.

Click the Index or Contents tabs, as appropriate, and then follow the relevant steps.

Using Index
Do the following:

Type in a word or phrase

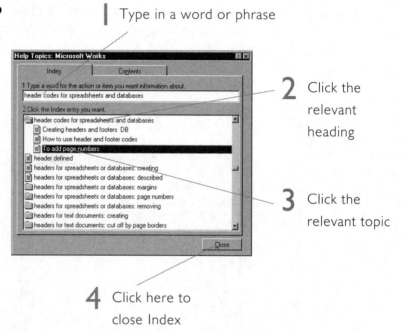

2 Click the relevant heading

3 Click the relevant topic

4 Click here to close Index

After step 2, Works launches a series of sub-headings. When you find the topic you want information on (prefixed by ▤ instead of ▢), follow step 3. (For what happens after step 3, see page 33.)

Finally, carry out step 4.

Using the separate HELP window

When you've used the Contents or Index sections of HELP to pick the topic you want help with, Works normally displays it as a separate window by the side of the open document. Carry out steps 1-4 below, as appropriate:

HELP topic | Click here for a list of related topics

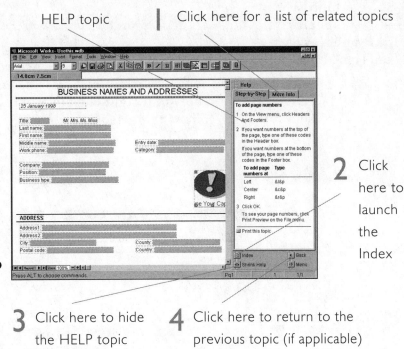

REMEMBER

When you carry out step 3, the open document expands to fill the document window.

2 Click here to launch the Index

3 Click here to hide the HELP topic

4 Click here to return to the previous topic (if applicable)

Sometimes, selecting a topic in the Index or Contents sections of the HELP system produces a different window:

HANDY TIP

Click any link (denoted by underlining, and coloured green) to display a special HELP box providing further information.

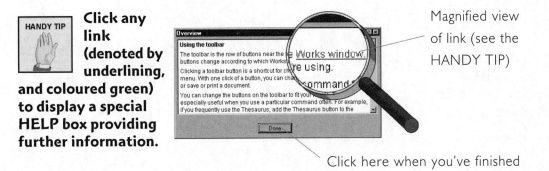

Magnified view of link (see the HANDY TIP)

Click here when you've finished

Other ways to get assistance

There are more immediate ways to get help:

Works calls these highly specific HELP bubbles 'ToolTips'.

- moving the mouse pointer over Toolbar buttons produces an explanatory HELP bubble:

- Fields in dialogs have associated Help boxes. To view a box, first right-click in a field. Then carry out the following procedure:

Left-click here for a
context-specific Help topic

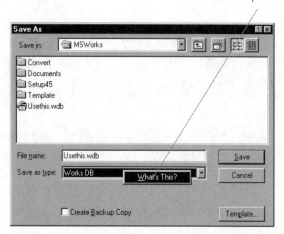

When you've finished with a Help box, press Esc to close it.

Works now launches a HELP box:

Specifies the type of file you are saving. The list includes all the available file types that this program can recognize.

Other standard Windows HELP features are also present; see your Windows documentation for how to use these.

The Word Processor

Chapter Two

This chapter gives you the basics of using the Word Processor. You'll learn how to enter text and negotiate the screen. You'll also discover how to format text/apply Easy Formats. Finally, you'll learn how to insert images with the ClipArt Gallery, and then customise page layout/printing.

Covers

The Word Processor screen

Below is an illustration of the Word Processor screen.

Title bar   Menu bar

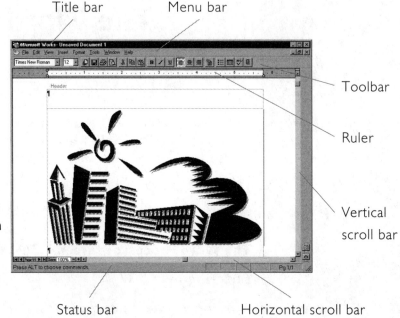

Toolbar

Ruler

Vertical
scroll bar

The Status bar displays information relating to the active document (e.g. what page you're on, and the total number of pages).

Status bar   Horizontal scroll bar

Some of these – e.g. the ruler and scroll bars – are standard to just about all programs which run under Windows. A few of them can be hidden, if required.

Specifying which screen components display

Pull down the View menu. Then do either of the following:

The ✔ signifies that the menu item is currently visible.

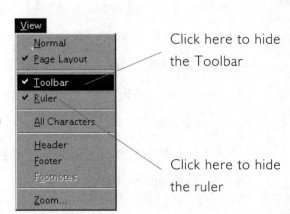

Click here to hide
the Toolbar

Click here to hide
the ruler

Entering text

The Word Processor has automatic word wrap. This means that you don't have to press Return to enter text on a new line: a new line is automatically started for you, when required.

Only press Return if you need to begin a new paragraph.

The Word Processor lets you enter text immediately after you've started it. You enter text at the insertion point:

A magnified view of the text insertion point

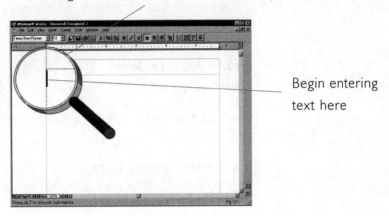

Begin entering text here

To count the number of words in the current Word Processor document, pull down the Tools menu and click Word Count.

Finally, click OK.

Overtyping selected text

By default, if you select text and then begin typing, Works replaces this with the new text automatically. This is often a useful way to work with documents. However, you can turn off this feature. When you do this, new text is positioned *in front of* the specified text.

Pull down the Tools menu and click Options. Do the following:

To word-count specific paragraphs, pre-select them. Pull down the Tools menu and click Word Count.

Finally, click OK.

Ensure this tab is active

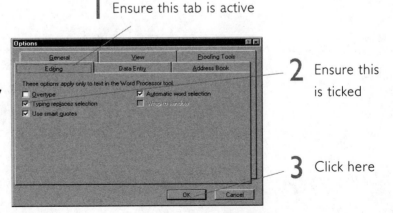

2 Ensure this is ticked

3 Click here

Moving around in documents

You can use the following to move through Word Processor documents:

- keystrokes

- the vertical/horizontal scroll bars

- the Go To dialog

Using keystrokes

Works implements the standard Windows direction keys. Use the left, right, up and down cursor keys in the usual way. Additionally, Home, End, Page Up and Page Down work normally.

Using the scroll bars

Use your mouse to perform any of the following actions;

Click anywhere here to jump to the left or right

Click anywhere here to jump to another location in the document

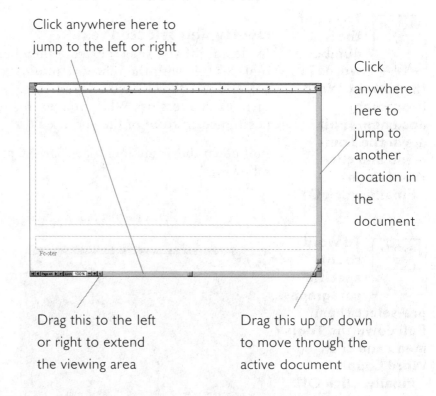

Footer

Drag this to the left or right to extend the viewing area

Drag this up or down to move through the active document

...contd

 You can use either of two keyboard shortcuts to launch the Go To dialog. Simply press Ctrl+G, or F5.

Using the Go To dialog

You can use the Go To dialog to move to any page number within the open document.

Pull down the Edit menu and click Go To. Now do the following:

1 Type in the number of the page you want to jump to

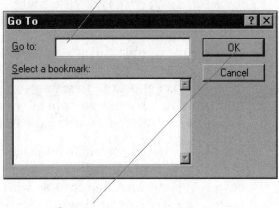

2 Click here

 To insert a bookmark into a document, place the insertion point at the relevant location. Pull down the Edit menu and click Bookmark. In the Name field in the Bookmark Name dialog, type in a name. Click OK.

You can also use the Go To dialog to move to a pre-inserted bookmark. Bookmarks are hidden place markers which you can insert into documents at important locations (for instance, in text which you want to revise later, or where you want to add clip art). For how to insert a bookmark, see the tip on the left.

Once you've inserted one or more bookmarks, you can then have the Word Processor jump to the bookmark of your choice.

Launch the Go To dialog, as above. Don't follow step 1 above; instead, in the Select a bookmark field, click the bookmark you want to jump to. Then carry out step 2.

Using views

The Word Processor module lets you examine your work in various ways, according to the approach you need. It calls these 'views'.

There are two principal views:

Normal

Normal View is used for basic text editing. In Normal View, most formatting elements are still visible; for instance, coloured, emboldened or italicised text displays faithfully. Line and page breaks, tabs and paragraph alignments/formatting will display. On the other hand, little attempt is made to show document structure or layout; for example, inserted clip art images invariably display on the left of the page, and headers and footers are invisible except on the first page of the document. Additionally, text will probably display on screen in a way which bears little relation to how it will print.

For these reasons, Normal View is quick and easy to use. It's suitable for bulk text entry and editing. It isn't, however, recommended for use with graphics (for this, switch to Page Layout view – see below).

Page Layout

Page Layout – the default – view works like Normal view, with one exception: the positioning of items on the page is reproduced accurately. What you see is a reasonable representation of what your document will look like when printed. Headers and footers are visible, and can be edited directly; margins display faithfully; and pictures occupy their correct position on-screen.

In Page Layout view, the screen is updated more slowly. As a result, use it when your document is nearing completion, for final proofing. This suggestion is particularly apt if you're working with a slow computer.

There is a third view which you'll use frequently: Print Preview. See later in this section for more information.

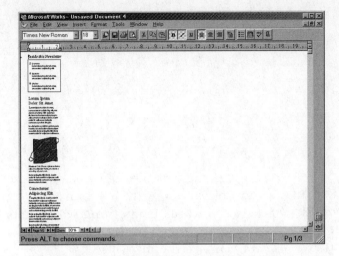

Normal
view

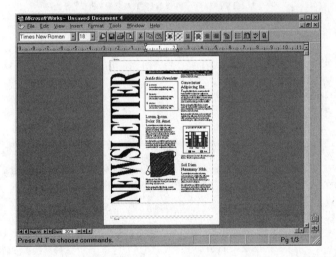

Page
Layout
view

Switching between Normal & Page Layout views

Pull down the View menu. Click Normal or Page Layout, as appropriate (the view which is currently active has ✔ against it).

Viewing special characters

The Word Processor has a special view mode whereby special characters:

- hyphens
- non-breaking spaces
- paragraph marks
- spaces

HANDY TIP

To enter special characters (e.g. paragraph marks and non-breaking hyphens), do the following.

At the relevant location in your document, pull down the Edit menu and click Special Character. In the Select a character: box in the Insert Special Character dialog, click a character.

Finally, click OK.

can be made visible. This is sometimes useful. For example, if you want to ensure there are no double spaces between words (something which happens surprisingly often), it's much easier to delete the unwanted spaces if you can see them.

Viewing hidden characters

Pull down the View menu and click All Characters.

The illustration below shows a magnified view of 2 (normally invisible) characters:

Spaces

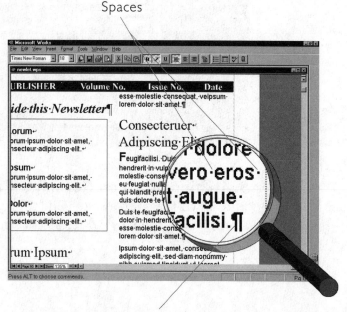

Paragraph mark symbol

Changing zoom levels

The ability to vary the level of magnification for the active document is often useful. Sometimes, it's helpful to 'zoom out' (i.e. decrease the magnification) so that you can take an overview; at other times, you'll need to 'zoom in' (increase the magnification) to work in greater detail. The Word Processor module lets you do either of these very easily.

You can do either of the following:

- choose from preset zoom levels (e.g. 100%, 75%)

- specify your own zoom percentage

- choose a zoom setting based on document margins

Setting the zoom level

Pull down the View menu and click Zoom. Now carry out step 1, 2 or 3 below. Then follow step 4:

Click a preset zoom level

Re step 2 –
entries
here must
lie in the
following range:
25%-1000%

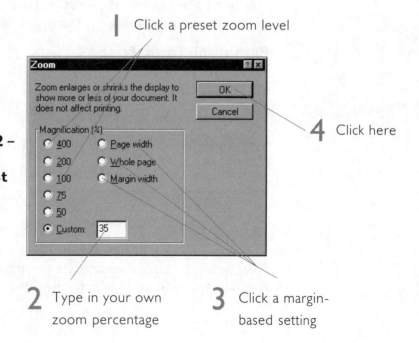

4 Click here

2 Type in your own zoom percentage

3 Click a margin-based setting

Formatting text – an overview

The Word Processor lets you format text in a variety of ways. Very broadly, however, and for the sake of convenience, text formatting can be divided into two overall categories:

Character formatting

Character formatting is concerned with altering the *appearance* of selected text. Examples include:

- changing the font

- changing the type size

- colouring text

- changing the font style (bold, italic, underlining etc.)

- applying font effects (superscript and subscript)

Character formatting is a misnomer in one sense: it can also be applied to specified paragraphs of text, or to parts of specified paragraphs.

Paragraph formatting

Paragraph formatting has to do with the structuring and layout of paragraphs of text. Examples include:

- specifying paragraph indents

- specifying paragraph alignment (e.g. left or right justification)

- specifying paragraph and line spacing

- imposing borders and/or fills on paragraphs

The Word Processor has a useful text formatting shortcut: Easy Formats. Easy Formats are pre-defined collections of formatting commands which you can apply to selected text in one go.

Changing the font and/or type size

Character formatting can be changed in two ways:

* from within the Font dialog

* (to a lesser extent) by using the Toolbar

Works uses standard Windows procedures for text selection.

Applying a new font or type size (1)

First, select the text whose typeface and/or type size you want to amend. Pull down the Format menu and click Font and Style. Now carry out steps 1 and/or 2 below. Finally, follow step 3:

Click a font

Re step 2 – as well as whole point sizes, you can also enter half-point increments; i.e. the Word Processor will accept: 10, 10.5 or 11 **but not:** 10.75 or 11.2

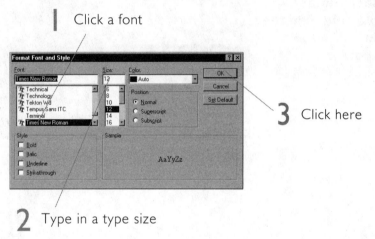

3 Click here

2 Type in a type size

Applying a new font or type size (2)

Make sure the Toolbar is visible. Now select the text you want to amend and do the following:

If the Toolbar isn't currently visible, pull down the View menu and click Toolbar.

Click here; select the font you want to use in the drop-down list

Type in the type size you need and press Enter

Changing text colour

You can only change the colour of text by using the Font dialog.

First, select the text you want to alter. Pull down the Format dialog and click Font. Now do the following:

Re step 1 – clicking Auto sets the colour to black (unless you've amended the default Windows text colour).

Click here

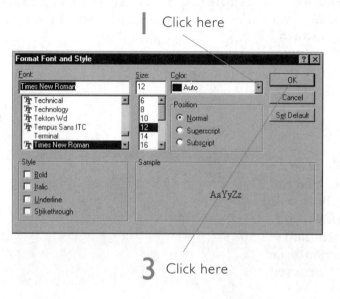

3 Click here

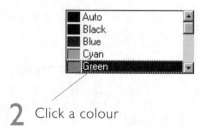

2 Click a colour

Removing colours from text

You can use a shortcut to return text to black. First, select the coloured text. Then press Ctrl+Spacebar.

If the text has had style enhancements (e.g. italicisation) or effects (e.g. superscript) applied to it, these are also removed.

Changing the font style

In the Word Processor, the following styles are available:

- **Bold**

- *Italic*

- <u>Underline</u>

- ~~Strikethrough~~

You can use the Font dialog or the Toolbar to change font styles.

You can also use keyboard shortcuts:

Ctrl + B   Emboldens text

Ctrl + I   Italicises text

Ctrl + U   Underlines text

Amending the font style (1)

First, select the text whose style you want to change. Then pull down the Format menu and click Font. Do the following:

The Sample section provides an indication of what the amendments you make look like.

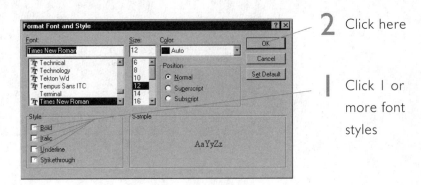

2 Click here

I Click I or more font styles

Amending the font style (2)

First, select the relevant text. Ensure the Toolbar is visible. Then carry out any of the following:

If the Toolbar isn't visible, pull down the View menu and click Toolbar.

Click here to embolden the text

Click here to underline the text

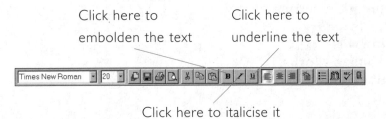

Click here to italicise it

Font effects

You can use the following font effects in the Word Processor:

- Superscript – e.g. f^{ont effect}

- Subscript – e.g. f_{ont effect}

HANDY TIP You can also use the following keyboard shortcuts:

Ctrl + +   Superscript
Ctrl + =   Subscript

Applying font effects

First, select the relevant text. Pull down the Format dialog and click Font. Then carry out the following steps:

2 Click here

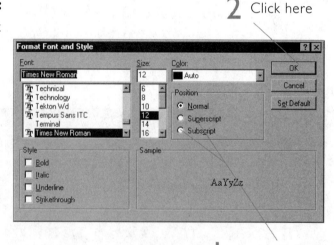

Click the relevant option

HANDY TIP The **Superscript and Subscript** buttons can be found in the Format menu category within the Customize Works Toolbar dialog.

Using the Toolbar to apply effects

As it ships, the Works Toolbar *won't* let you superscript or subscript text. However, you can add buttons for these functions easily and quickly.

For how to do this, see page 11.

Indenting paragraphs – an overview

You can achieve a similar effect by using tabs. However, indents are easier to apply (and amend subsequently).

Indents are a crucial component of document layout. For instance, in most document types indenting the first line of paragraphs (i.e. moving it inwards away from the left page margin) makes the text much more legible.

Other document types – e.g. bibliographies – can use the following:

- hanging indents (where the first line is unaltered, while subsequent lines are indented)

- full indents (where the entire paragraph is indented away from the left and/or the right margins)

Some of the potential indent combinations are shown in the illustration below:

Don't confuse indents with page margins.
  Margins are the gap between the edge of the page and the text area; indents define the distance between the margins and text.

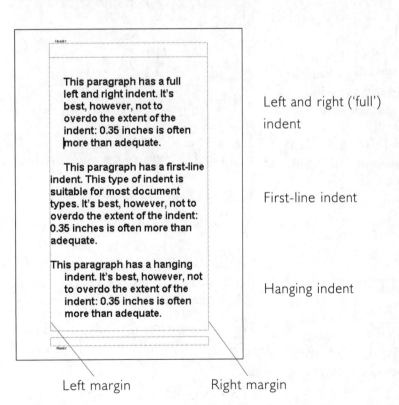

This paragraph has a full left and right indent. It's best, however, not to overdo the extent of the indent: 0.35 inches is often more than adequate.

    This paragraph has a first-line indent. This type of indent is suitable for most document types. It's best, however, not to overdo the extent of the indent: 0.35 inches is often more than adequate.

This paragraph has a hanging indent. It's best, however, not to overdo the extent of the indent: 0.35 inches is often more than adequate.

Left and right ('full') indent

First-line indent

Hanging indent

Left margin   Right margin

Applying indents to paragraphs

Paragraphs can be indented from within the Paragraph dialog, or (to a lesser extent) by using the Toolbar (if you add extra buttons to it).

Indenting text (1)

First, select the paragraph(s) you want to indent. Pull down the Format menu and click Paragraph. Now follow step 1 below. If you want a left indent, carry out step 2. For a right indent, follow step 3. To achieve a first-line or hanging indent, follow step 4. Finally, irrespective of the indent type, carry out step 5.

Ensure this tab is active

HANDY TIP

Re step 4 – to implement a hanging indent, type in a negative value e.g: -0.35 **and the equivalent value in the Left field e.g:** -0.35

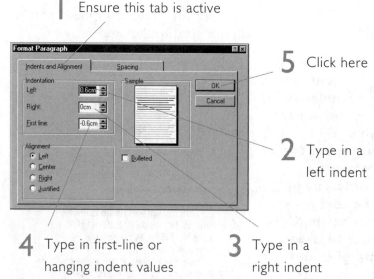

5 Click here

2 Type in a left indent

4 Type in first-line or hanging indent values

3 Type in a right indent

Using the Toolbar to apply effects

As it ships, the Works Toolbar *won't* let you indent text. However, you can add the following buttons:

HANDY TIP

These buttons can be found within the Format menu category in the Customize Works Toolbar dialog.

  Moves the indent out one level

  Moves the indent in one level

For how to do this, see page 11.

Aligning paragraphs

You can use the following types of alignment:

Left	Text is flush with the left page margin
Center	Text aligns equidistantly between the left and right page margins
Right	Text is flush with the right page margin
Justified	Text is flush with the left *and* right page margins

You can align text from within the Paragraph dialog, or (to a lesser extent) with the use of the Toolbar.

 You can only use the Toolbar to justify text if you add a special button ▤ **to it:**
   This is found in the Format menu category within the Customize Works Toolbar dialog. (See page 11).

Aligning text (1)

First, select the paragraph you want to indent. Pull down the Format menu and click Paragraph. Now:

Ensure this tab is active

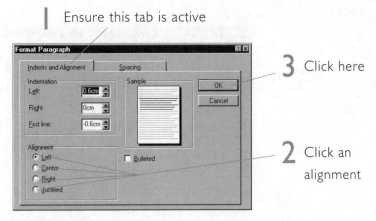

3 Click here

2 Click an alignment

 If the Toolbar isn't currently visible, pull down the View menu and click Toolbar.

Aligning text (2)

Select the relevant paragraph(s). Then click any of these:

Left align   Right align

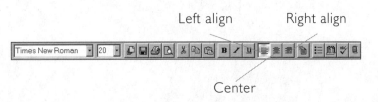

Center

Specifying paragraph spacing

You can customise the vertical space before and/or after specific text paragraphs.

By default, Works defines paragraph spacing in terms of lines, e.g. 6li (6 lines). However, if you want you can enter measurements in different units. To do this, apply any of the following suffixes to values you enter:

As a general rule, set low paragraph spacing settings: a little goes a long way.

- in (for inches e.g. 2 in)

- cm (for centimetres e.g. 5 cm)

- pt (for points e.g. 14 pt)

Applying paragraph spacing (1)

72 points are roughly equivalent to one inch. The Word Processor also uses points to measure type sizes.

First, select the paragraph whose spacing you want to adjust. Pull down the Format menu and click Paragraph. Now carry out the steps below:

| Ensure this tab is active

4 Click here

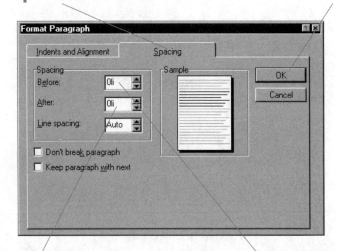

3 Type in the amount of post-paragraph spacing you need

2 Type in the amount of pre-paragraph spacing you need

Line spacing – an overview

It's often necessary to amend line spacing. This is the vertical distance between individual lines of text, or more accurately between the baseline (the imaginary line on which text appears to sit) of one line and the baseline of the previous.

Line spacing is also known as leading (pronounced 'ledding').

The Word Processor lets you apply the following line spacing setting:

Auto   Each line is as high as the tallest character in it.

Alternatively, you can:

- specify the number of lines which should be applied as the line spacing (e.g. 4li – four lines)

- specify a number followed by a measurement in inches, centimetres or points (e.g. 0.5 in, 3 cm or 12 pt)

You can use the following keyboard shortcuts to adjust line spacing:

Ctrl + 1   Single spacing
Ctrl + 5   1½ spacing
Ctrl + 2   Double spacing

This paragraph is in single line spacing. Newspapers frequently use this.

Single line spacing

This paragraph is in 1½ line spacing. Probably no one uses this, but it serves as a useful illustration.

1.5 line spacing

This paragraph is in double line spacing; writers use this when preparing manuscripts

Double line spacing

Adjusting line spacing

First, select the relevant paragraph(s). Then pull down the Format menu and do the following:

HANDY TIP If you've just created a new document, you can set the line spacing before you begin to enter text.

Simply leave the insertion point at the start of the document, and then follow the procedures outlined here.

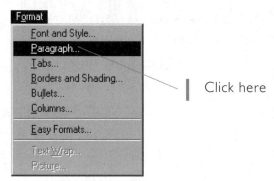

Click here

Now perform steps 2 to 4 below:

2 Ensure this tab is active

4 Click here

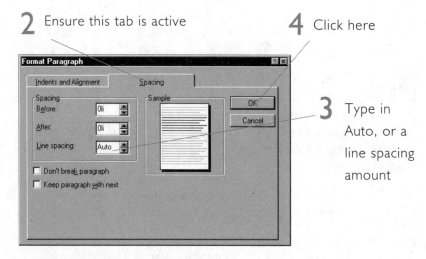

3 Type in Auto, or a line spacing amount

HANDY TIP These buttons can be found within the Format menu category in the Customize Works Toolbar dialog.

For how to implement these buttons, see page 11.

A shortcut...

As it ships, the Works Toolbar *won't* let you adjust line spacing. However, you can add buttons for the following functions easily and quickly:

 Single line spacing

 Double line spacing

Working with columns

The Word Processor module lets you arrange text into columns. You can:

- insert multiple columns

- specify the inter-column gap

- have Works insert a vertical line between columns

When you insert columns, they apply to the entire document.

Applying columns

Place the insertion point anywhere within the current Word Processor document. Pull down the Format menu and do the following:

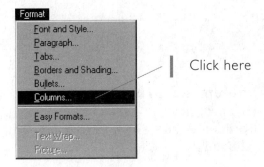

Click here

Re step 2 – the number of columns you can insert depends on:
- your margin settings
- the amount of inter-column gap

2 Type in the no. of columns

5 Click here

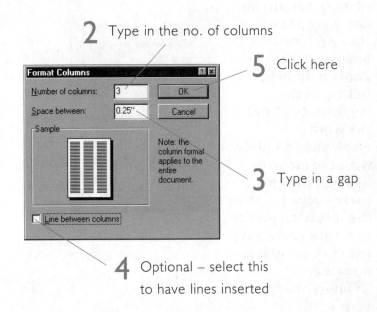

3 Type in a gap

4 Optional – select this to have lines inserted

Automatic hyphenation

 BEWARE

The results of having Works apply automatic hyphenation can sometimes be unacceptable.

For example, if the word:

carrying

were hyphenated to:

car-

rying

you might feel the fact that 'car' is a word in its own right distracting...

To correct this, press Ctrl+Z *immediately*. Rerun hyphenation on the suspect paragraph. Carry out step 1; in step 2 overleaf, however, ensure the Confirm field is ticked. In the Hyphenate at field, the word is displayed complete with the incorrect hyphen; use the cursor keys to move the insertion point to where you want the revised hyphen inserted.

Finally, carry out step 3.

Text – particularly text which is fully justified (see page 51) – can often look unattractive and lack legibility. This is because Works increases the gaps between words in order to achieve justification. The solution is to implement the Word Processor's automatic hyphenation feature, usually for the whole document or – alternatively – for selected paragraphs.

When automatic hyphenation is in force, and when it determines that a sentence requires it, the Word Processor module:

- breaks the final word

- inserts a hyphen

- carries over the final part of the word to the start of the next sentence

Implementing hyphenation

If appropriate, pre-select the paragraph(s) you want to hyphenate. Pull down the Tools menu and do the following:

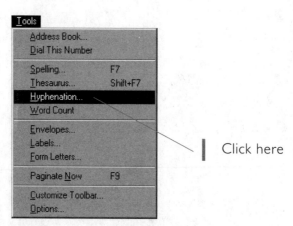

Click here

Now carry out the following additional steps:

Re step 2 – when Confirm is deselected, the ✔ is not present.

2 Ensure this is deselected

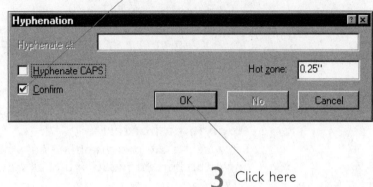

3 Click here

In the illustration below, the higher paragraph shows justified text without hyphenation; in the second, however, hyphenation has been applied:

> This is an example of text which has been badly laid. Notice that, because it is justified (fully aligned with the left and right page edges), Works increases the spaces between words. However, this can sometimes produce an effect which looks unattractive and even clumsy.
>
> Compare the above with the following:
>
> This is an example of text which has been hyphenated. Notice that, although Works has increased the spaces between words because of the justification, any words which fall within a 'hot zone' (a given area measured from the right page edge - by default, 0.25 inches) are automatically hyphenated if this is appropriate. This results in text being easier to read, and more aesthetically pleasing.

Paragraph borders

By default, the Word Processor does not border paragraph text. However, you can apply a wide selection of borders if you want. You can specify:

- the border type

- the border thickness

- how many sides the border should have

- the border colour

- whether the bordered text should have a drop shadow

Applying a border

First, select the paragraph(s) you want to border. Then pull down the Format menu and click Borders and Shading. Now do the following:

 The Sample area displays a preview of what your border combination will look like.

 Re step 4 – click Outline to have all 4 sides bordered. Or click Outline with shadow to impose a drop shadow, too. Then proceed as normal.

Ensure this tab is active

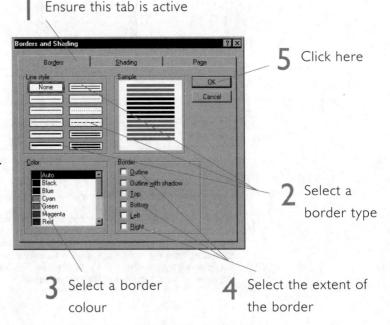

5 Click here

2 Select a border type

3 Select a border colour

4 Select the extent of the border

Paragraph fills

By default, the Word Processor does not apply a fill to text paragraphs. However, you can do the following if you want:

- apply a simple fill

- apply a simple pattern

- specify the foreground fill colour

- specify the background fill colour

Applying a fill

First, select the paragraph(s) you want to fill. Then pull down the Format menu and click Borders and Shading. Now carry out step 1 below. Follow steps 2, 3 and/or 4 as appropriate. Finally, carry out step 5:

The Sample area displays a preview of what your fill combination will look like.

1 Ensure this tab is active

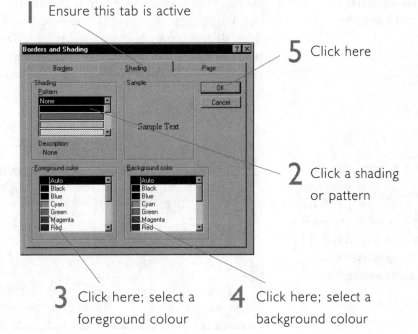

5 Click here

2 Click a shading or pattern

3 Click here; select a foreground colour

4 Click here; select a background colour

Working with tabs

Tabs are a means of indenting the first line of text paragraphs (you can also use indents for this purpose – see pages 49-50).

Never use the Space Bar to indent paragraphs. The result of doing so is at best uneven, because spaces vary in size according to the typeface and type size applying to specific paragraphs.

When you press the Tab key while the text insertion point is at the start of a paragraph, the text in the first line jumps to the next tab stop. This is a useful way to increase the legibility of your text. The Word Processor lets you set tab stops with great precision.

By default, tab stops are inserted automatically every half an inch. If you want, however, you can enter new or revised tab stop positions individually.

Setting tab stops

First, select the paragraph(s) in which you need to set tab stops. Pull down the Format menu and click Tabs. Now carry out step 1 below. If you want to implement a new default tab stop position, follow step 2. If you need to set up individual tab stops, carry out steps 3 and 4 as often as necessary. Finally, follow step 5 to confirm your changes.

When you've performed steps 3 & 4, the individual tab stop position appears here:

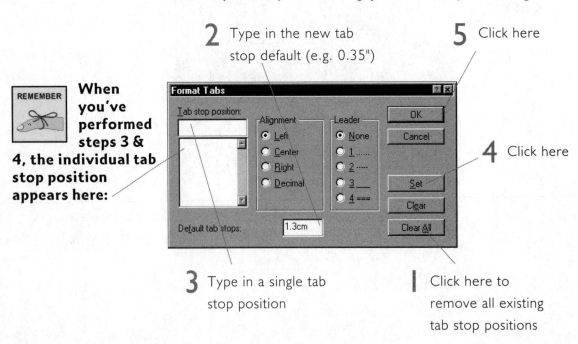

2 Type in the new tab stop default (e.g. 0.35")

5 Click here

3 Type in a single tab stop position

4 Click here

Click here to remove all existing tab stop positions

Searching for text

REMEMBER

The Works wildcard is very useful: it stands for *any* character. For instance, searching for me?t **would find:** meet **or** meat. **See 'Entering codes' below for more information.**

The Word Processor lets you search for specific text within the active document.

You can also search for special characters. For example, you can look for paragraph marks, tabs, wildcards, question marks, page breaks and spaces.

You can also:

- limit the search to words which match the case of the text you specify (e.g. if you search for 'Arm', Works will not flag 'arm' or 'ARM')

- limit the search to whole words (e.g. if you search for 'eat', Works will not flag 'beat' or 'meat')

Initiating a text search

Pull down the Edit menu and click Find. Now do the following:

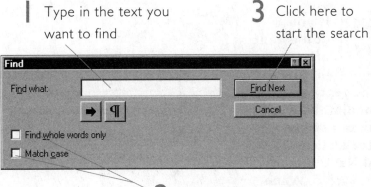

HANDY TIP

You can use a keyboard shortcut to launch the Find dialog. Simply press Ctrl+F.

1 Type in the text you want to find

3 Click here to start the search

2 Activate one or both of these, as appropriate

Entering codes

When you complete step 1, you can enter the following:

^w	Space	^d	Page break
^t	Tab	?	Wildcard
^p	Paragraph mark	^?	Question mark

Replacing text

When you've located text, you can have the Word Processor replace it automatically with the text of your choice.

You can customise find-and-replace operations with the same parameters as a simple Find operation. For example, you can make them case-specific, or only replace whole words. You can also incorporate a variety of codes (for how to do this, see the 'Searching for text' topic on the previous page).

There is, however, one exception to this: for obvious reasons, wildcards can't be incorporated in replacement text.

Initiating a find-and-replace operation

First pull down the Edit menu and click Replace. Now follow steps 1 and 2 below. Carry out step 3, as appropriate. Finally, follow step 4 (or see the REMEMBER tip):

HANDY TIP

You can use a keyboard shortcut here. **Simply press Ctrl+H.**

REMEMBER

If you don't want *all* instances of the text replaced immediately, don't carry out step 4. Instead, click the Find Next button after step 3. When the first match has been found, click Replace.
  Repeat this as often as necessary.

1 Type in the text you want to find

2 Type in the replacement text

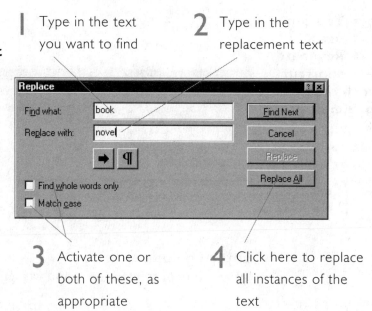

3 Activate one or both of these, as appropriate

4 Click here to replace all instances of the text

Working with headers

You can have the Word Processor print text at the top of each page within a document; the area of the page where repeated text appears is called the 'header'. In the same way, you can have text printed at the base of each page; in this case, the relevant page area is called the 'footer'. Headers and footers are printed within the top and bottom page margins, respectively.

REMEMBER

To edit an *existing* header, simply follow the procedures outlined here; in step 1, amend the current header text as necessary.

Inserting a header

In Normal view, move to the top of the first page, then click in the Header (H) area. Alternatively, in Page Layout view move to the top of the relevant page and click in the Header area.

Now do the following:

HANDY TIP

Re step 1 – you can have the Word Processor insert a special code which automatically inserts the page number in the header.

To do this, pull down the Insert menu and click Page Number.

Type in the Header text

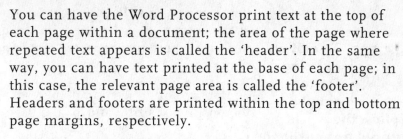

The Header area in Page Layout view

HANDY TIP

Header text can be formatted in the normal way. For instance, you can apply a new font and/or type size.

Click back in the main body of the document when you've finished creating the header.

Working with footers

You can have the Word Processor automatically print text at the bottom of each page within a document. The area of the page where this repeated text appears is called the 'footer'.

Footers are often used to display an abbreviated version of the document's title and/or the page number.

Inserting a footer

In Normal view, move to the top of the first page then click in the Footer (F) area. Alternatively, in Page Layout view move to the bottom of the relevant page and click in the Footer area.

Then do the following:

To edit an *existing* footer, simply follow the procedures outlined here; in step 1, amend the current footer text as necessary.

Re step 1 – you can have the Word Processor insert a special code which automatically inserts the page number in the footer.
  To do this, pull down the Insert menu and click Page Number.

Footer text can be formatted in the normal way. For instance, you can apply a new font and/or type size.

Type in the Footer text

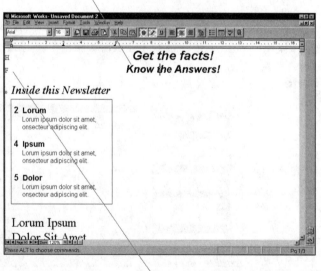

The Footer area in Normal view

Click back in the main body of the document when you've finished creating the footer.

Undo and redo

The Word Processor lets you reverse – 'undo' – just about any editing operation. If, in the event, you decide that you *do* want to proceed with an operation which you've reversed, you can 'redo' it. In effect, this amounts to undoing an undo.

You can undo and redo actions in the following ways (in descending order of complexity):

- via the keyboard

- from within the Edit menu

- from within the Toolbar

Using the keyboard
Simply press Ctrl+Z to undo an action. If you want to reinstate it immediately afterwards, press Ctrl+Z again.

Using the Edit menu
Pull down the Edit menu and do the following:

Click here

Using the Toolbar
As it ships, the Works Toolbar *won't* let you undo or redo operations. However, you can add the following button easily and quickly:

 Undo/redo button

Easy Formats – an overview

The Word Processor module comes with a selection of pre-defined Easy Formats. Examples are:

- Boxed text

- Contemporary masthead

- Cursive note

- Flyer text

- Hanging indent

- List with lines

- Quotation

- Title page

Easy Formats are named collections of associated formatting commands. The advantage of using Easy Formats is that you can apply more than one formatting enhancement to selected text in one go. Another advantage is the professional quality of the results.

You can easily create your own Easy Formats for later use.

In the illustration below, the Contemporary masthead Easy Format has been applied to a document created with the Letterhead TaskWizard:

The illustration below shows the document before the Easy Format was applied:

The original (plain) masthead area

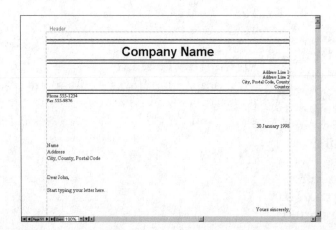

Creating an Easy Format

The easiest way to create an Easy Format is to:

A. apply the appropriate formatting enhancements to specific text and then select it

B. tell Works to save this formatting as an Easy Format

First, carry out step A above. Then pull down the Format menu and click Easy Formats. Now do the following:

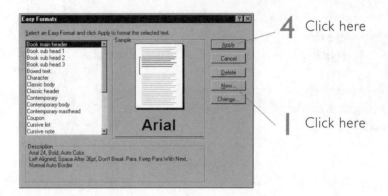

4 Click here

1 Click here

2 Type in a name for your Easy Format

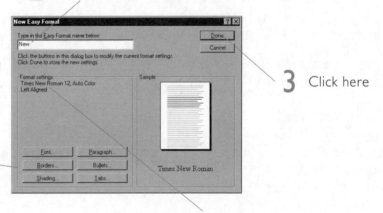

3 Click here

HANDY TIP

If you want to adjust the formatting of your new Easy Format, click any of the buttons in this section of the dialog: *after* **step 2.**
Complete the dialog which launches in the normal way.
Finally, carry out steps 3 and 4.

Brief description of formatting associated with the new Easy Format

See 'Applying an Easy Format' to use your new format.

Applying an Easy Format

Applying Easy Formats is easy.

First, select the text you want to apply the Easy Format to. Or, if you only want to apply it to a single paragraph, place the insertion point inside it. Pull down the Format menu and click Easy Formats. Now do the following:

Click an Easy Format

Works displays brief details of the selected Easy Format here:

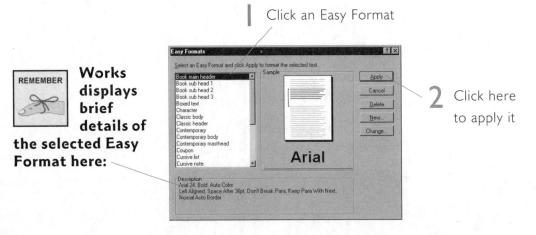

2 Click here to apply it

Shortcut for applying Easy Formats

Works makes it even easier to apply Easy Formats if you currently have the Toolbar on-screen. (If you haven't, pull down the View menu and click Toolbar).

Re step 2 – if the Easy Format you want to apply isn't listed, click More Easy Formats in the menu. This launches the Easy Formats dialog.
  Complete this in line with the instructions above.

Select the text you want to apply the format to. Then do the following:

Click here

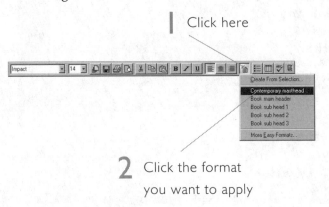

2 Click the format you want to apply

Amending an Easy Format

You can easily adjust the formatting associated with existing Easy Formats.

Pull down the Format menu and click Easy Formats. Now carry out the following steps:

1 Select the Easy Format you want to amend

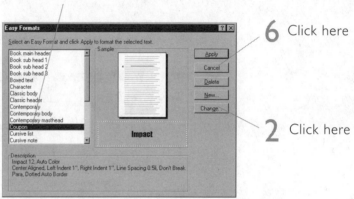

6 Click here

2 Click here

3 Rename the Easy Format, if required

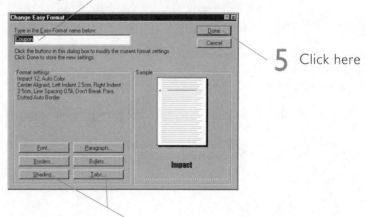

5 Click here

4 Click any of these buttons, then complete the dialog which launches

Deleting Easy Formats

Good housekeeping sometimes makes it necessary to remove unwanted Easy Formats (after all, there's no point retaining an Easy Format if you're never likely to use it, especially if you're short of hard disk space). The Word Processor lets you do this very easily.

Removing an Easy Format

Pull down the Format menu and click Easy Formats. Now carry out the following steps:

1 | Select an Easy Format

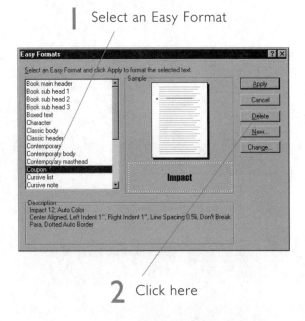

2 Click here

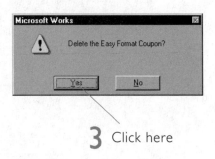

3 Click here

Spell-checking text

You can check for a variety of errors:

- misspellings
- incorrect capitalisations (e.g. 'THis' at the start of a sentence)
- repeated words (e.g. 'the the')

Works makes use of two separate dictionaries. One can be thought of as _yours_. When you follow step 4, the flagged word is stored in this and recognised in future checking sessions.

If the flagged word isn't correct and Works' suggestions are also wrong, type in the correct version in the Change To field. Then carry out step 2 or 3.

To check all the text within the active document in one go, pull down the Tools menu and click Spelling. Works starts spell-checking the document from the beginning. When it encounters a word it doesn't recognise, Works flags it and produces a special dialog (see below). Usually, it provides alternative suggestions; if one of these is correct, you can opt to have it replace the flagged word. You can do this singly (i.e. just this instance is replaced) or globally (where all future instances – within the current checking session – are replaced).

Alternatively, you can have Works:

- ignore _this_ instance of the flagged word and resume checking

- ignore _all_ future instances of the word and resume checking

- add the word to your personal dictionary and resume checking

Carry out step 1 below, then step 2 OR 3. Alternatively, perform any one of steps 4, 5 OR 6:

1 If a suggestion is correct, click it, then follow step 2 OR 3

5 Click here to ignore just this instance

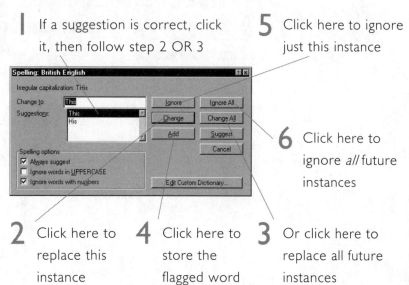

6 Click here to ignore _all_ future instances

2 Click here to replace this instance

4 Click here to store the flagged word

3 Or click here to replace all future instances

Searching for synonyms

The Word Processor lets you search for synonyms while you're editing the active document. You do this by calling up the resident Thesaurus. The Thesaurus categorises words into meanings, and each meaning is allocated various synonyms from which you can choose.

As a bonus, the Thesaurus also supplies:

HANDY TIP

You can also use a keyboard shortcut to launch the Thesaurus. Simply press Shift+F7.

- antonyms (e.g. if you look up 'good', Works lists 'abominable', 'bad', 'base' and 'corrupt')

- related words (e.g. if you look up 'inside', Works lists 'side' and 'aside')

Using the Thesaurus

First, select the word for which you require a synonym, antonym or related term. (Or simply position the insertion point within it). Pull down the Tools menu and click Thesaurus. Now do the following:

The selected word appears here

Thesaurus: British English		? ✕
Looked up:	Replace with synonym:	Replace
Inside	within	Look Up
Meanings:	within	Cancel
interior (noun)	inside of	
within (adv.)		
Antonyms		
Related words		

1 Click a meaning. Or click Antonyms or Related words, if appropriate

2 Click a replacement word

3 Click here to substitute the replacement word

Working with images

The Word Processor module lets you add colour or greyscale images to the active document. Images – also called graphics – include:

- drawings produced in other programs

- clip art

- scanned photographs

Use images – whatever their source – to add much needed visual impact to documents. But use them judiciously: too much colour can be off-putting, and ultimately self-defeating.

Images are stored in various third-party formats. These formats are organised into two basic types:

Bitmap images

Bitmaps consist of pixels (dots) arranged in such a way that they form a graphic image. Because of the very nature of bitmaps, the question of 'resolution' – the sharpness of an image expressed in dpi (dots per inch) – is very important. Bitmaps look best if they're displayed at their native resolution. Works can manipulate a wide variety of third-party bitmap graphics formats. These include: PCX, TIF, TGA and GIF.

Vector images

You can also insert vector graphics files into Word Processor documents. Vector images consist of and are defined by algebraic equations. They're less complex than bitmaps: they contain less detail. Vector files can also include bitmap information.

Irrespective of the format type, Works can incorporate images with the help of special 'filters'. These are special mini-programs whose job it is to translate third-party formats into a form which Works can use.

Brief notes on image formats

Works will happily import/export a wide selection of bitmap and vector graphic formats. These are some of the main formats:

Bitmap formats

PCX   An old standby. Originated with PC Paintbrush, a paint program. Used for years to transfer graphics data between Windows applications. Supports compression.

TIFF   Tagged Image File Format. Suffix: .TIF. If anything, even more widely used than PCX, across a whole range of platforms and applications. Supports numerous types and levels of compression.

BMP   Not as common as PCX and TIFF, but still popular. One drawback: sometimes, compression isn't available.

TGA   Targa. A high-end format, and also a bridge with so-called low-end computers (e.g. Amiga and Atari). Often used in PC and Mac paint and ray-tracing programs because of its high-resolution colour fidelity. Supports compression.

GIF   Graphics Interchange Format. Developed for the on-line transmission of graphics data across the CompuServe network. Just about any Windows program – and a lot more besides – will read GIF. Disadvantage: it can't handle more than 256 colours. One of the few graphics formats which can be used in HTML (HyperText Markup Language) documents on the World Wide Web. Compression is supported.

PCD   (Kodak) PhotoCD. Used primarily to store photographs on CD.

JPEG   Joint Photographic Experts Group. Suffix: .JPG. Used on the PC and Mac for the storage and display of photographs. One of the few graphics formats which can be used in HTML (HyperText Markup Language) documents on the World Wide Web. A very high level of compression is built into the format.

Vector formats

CGM   Computer Graphics Metafile. Frequently used in the past, especially as a medium for clip-art transmission. Less frequently used nowadays.

Works will also import the following graphics files:

- .WPG WordPerfect)
- .CDR (CorelDRAW)

EPS   Encapsulated PostScript. Perhaps the most widely used PostScript format. Actually, PostScript (a programming language in its own right) combines vector *and* bitmap data very successfully. Incorporates a low-resolution bitmap 'header' for preview purposes. If you want to export to a vector format and have a choice, you'd be well advised to use EPS.

WMF   Windows Metafile. Similar to CGM, but even more frequently used. Used for information exchange between just about all Windows programs. Often produces files which are much smaller than the equivalent bitmaps (though not because of compression – there isn't any). If you need a vector format and can't use EPS, use WMF wherever possible.

The 7000+ clip art images supplied with Microsoft Works are in WMF format.

Inserting images – an overview

Works lets you insert the following into your word processor documents:

- clip art

- pictures

By clip art, Works means the image files supplied on the program CD, some of which will have been automatically copied to your hard disk during installation.

The term 'pictures', on the other hand, refers to third-party graphics formats (e.g. TIFF and PCX).

You add both clip art and pictures with the use of the Clip Gallery. The Clip Gallery:

— provides a visual category of clip art and pictures on your system

— lets you view images as 'thumbnails' (small icons representing clip art and pictures)

— makes it easy to keep track of clip art and pictures

REMEMBER

If you don't have the Works CD in your CD-ROM drive, far fewer categories display here:

HANDY TIP

In version 4, the Clip Gallery is known as the ClipArt Gallery, and is rather different.

The Clip Art Gallery displaying clip art images

...contd

In the Clip Gallery, clip art images are organised under a large number of categories. Examples are:

- Animals

- Backgrounds

- Borders & Frames

- Cartoons

- Gestures

- Food & Dining

- Home & Family

- Industry

- Metaphors

- Music

- Nature

- People at Work

- Science & Technology

- Weather

 HANDY TIP

If you don't have the Works CD in your CD-ROM drive, far fewer categories (and images) are available).

Because Works supplies so many clip art images, it's important to be able to carry out image housekeeping.

You can:

— allocate a different category to a given clip art image

— create new categories

— rename categories

Inserting clip art

Make sure the Works CD is in the relevant drive. Within the relevant Word Processor document, do the following:

| Click where you want the clip art inserted

 In version 4, a different procedure is required. Launch the ClipArt Gallery in the normal way. Click the Organize button. In the Organize ClipArt dialog, click the Add Picture button. Use the Add Pictures to ClipArt Gallery dialog to locate the picture you want to add; click it, then click Open.

Now follow steps 11-12 on page 82 to insert the image into the open document.

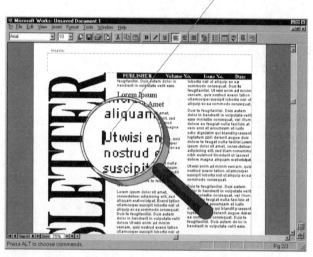

Pull down the Insert menu and do the following:

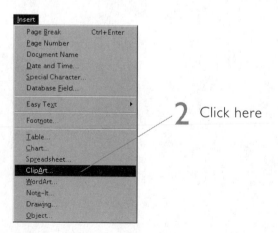

2 Click here

Now carry out the following additional steps:

3 Ensure this tab is active   **5** Select an image

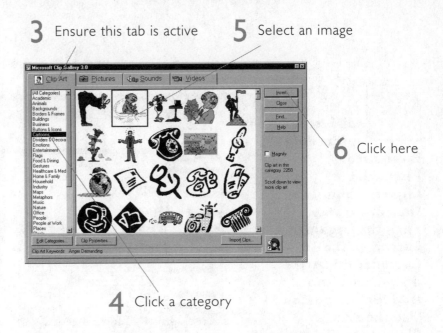

6 Click here

4 Click a category

The
inserted
image

Inserting pictures

Make sure the Works CD is in its drive. Within the relevant Word Processor document, do the following:

In version 4, a different procedure is required.
Launch the ClipArt Gallery in the normal way. Click the Organize button. In the Organize ClipArt dialog, click the Add Picture button. Use the Add Pictures to ClipArt Gallery dialog to locate the picture you want to add; click it, then click Open.
Now follow steps 11-12 on page 82 to insert the picture into the open document.

Click where you want the clip art inserted

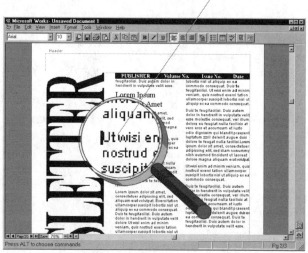

Pull down the Insert menu and do the following:

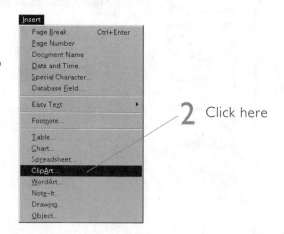

2 Click here

...contd

Now carry out the following additional steps:

3 Ensure this tab is active

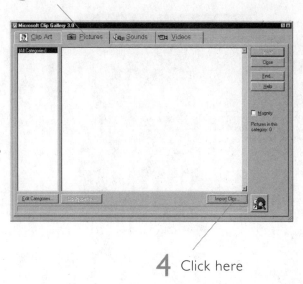

4 Click here

5 Click here. In the drop-down list, click the drive which hosts the picture

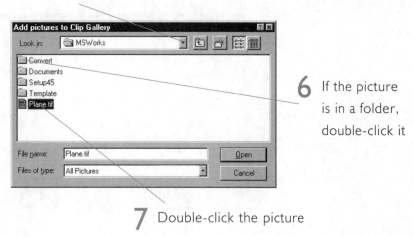

6 If the picture is in a folder, double-click it

7 Double-click the picture

...contd

Now carry out the following additional steps:

8 Optional – allocate a keyword

See the HANDY TIP on page 80 for how to insert pictures in version 4.

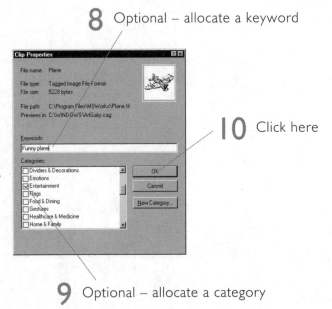

10 Click here

9 Optional – allocate a category

11 Click the image

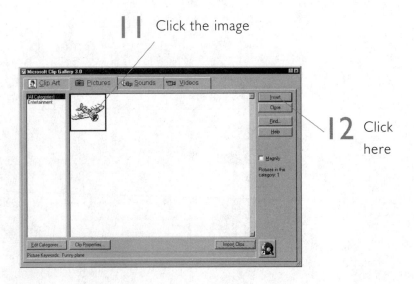

12 Click here

Gallery housekeeping

You can carry out housekeeping operations on categories.

Applying new categories to images

Launch the Clip Gallery in the usual way. Then do the following:

| Ensure either tab is active   2 Select an image

HANDY TIP

In version 4, a different procedure is required.
Launch the ClipArt Gallery in the normal way. Select an image, then click the Organize button. In the Organize ClipArt dialog, click the Picture Properties button. Use the dialog which launches to allocate one or more new categories.
Back in the Clip Art Gallery, click Close.

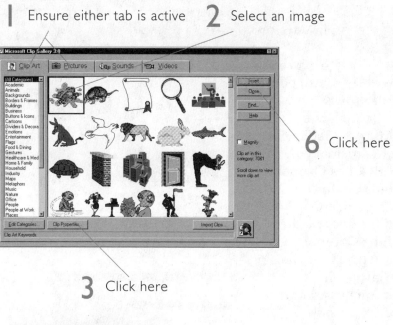

6 Click here

3 Click here

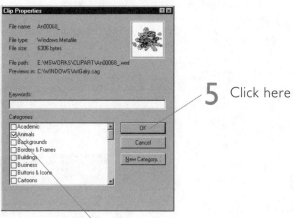

5 Click here

4 Allocate a (revised) category

Creating new image categories

Launch the Clip Gallery in the usual way. Then do the following:

In version 4, a different procedure is required.
Launch the ClipArt Gallery in the normal way. Click the Organize button. In the Organize ClipArt dialog, click the Edit Category List button. Use the dialog which launches to add one or more new categories.
Back in the Clip Art Gallery, click Close.

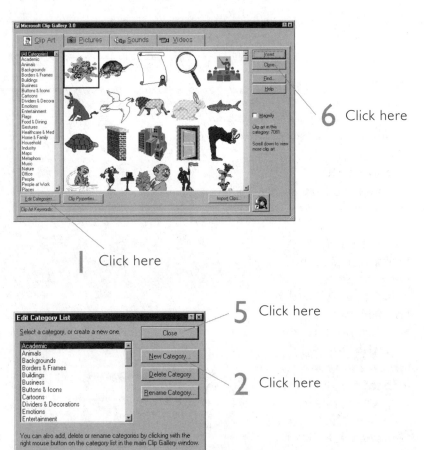

6 Click here

Click here

5 Click here

2 Click here

3 Name the new category

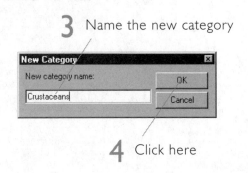

4 Click here

...contd

Renaming image categories

Launch the Clip Gallery in the usual way. Then do the following:

 In version 4, a different procedure is required. Launch the ClipArt Gallery in the normal way. Click the Organize button. In the Organize ClipArt dialog, click the Edit Category List button. Use the dialog which launches to select and rename a category. Back in the Clip Art Gallery, click Close.

HANDY TIP

7 Click here

1 Click here

2 Click a category

6 Click here

3 Click here

4 Rename the category

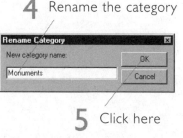

5 Click here

Manipulating images – an overview

Once you've inserted images into a document, you can work with them in a variety of ways. You can:

- rescale them

- specify how text flows around them

- apply a border

- move them

Selecting an image

To carry out any of these operations, you have to select the relevant image first. To do this, simply position the mouse pointer over the image and left-click once. Works surrounds the image with eight handles. These are positioned at the four corners, and midway on each side:

To have text align around – but not through – an image (Works calls this Text Wrap), select the image. Pull down the Format menu and click Picture. Activate the Text Wrap tab. Now click the following button:

Absolute

Finally, click OK.

Handles

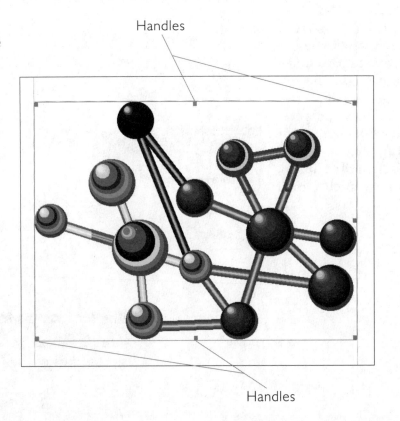

Handles

Rescaling images

There are two ways in which you can rescale images:

- proportionally, where the height/width ratio remains constant

- disproportionately, where the height/width ratio is disrupted (this is sometimes called 'warping' or 'skewing')

To rescale a image, first select it. Then move the mouse pointer over:

You can also use a special dialog to rescale images – see overleaf.

— one of the corner handles, if you want to rescale the image proportionally,

or

— one of the handles in the middle of the sides, if you want to warp it

In either eventuality, the mouse pointer changes to a double-headed arrow and the word 'RESIZE' appears below it. Click and hold down the left mouse button. Drag outwards to increase the image size or inwards to decrease it.

Release the mouse button to confirm the change.

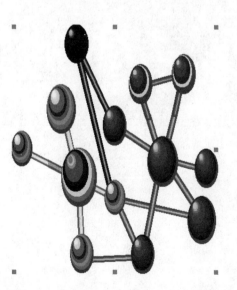

Here, the image from page 86 has been skewed from the right inwards

Rescaling images – the dialog route

You can use a special dialog to rescale images, a method which allows much greater precision.

First, select the image you want to amend. Pull down the Format menu and to the following:

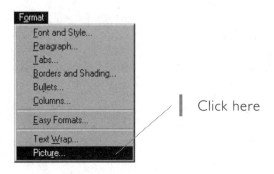

Click here

2 Ensure this tab is active

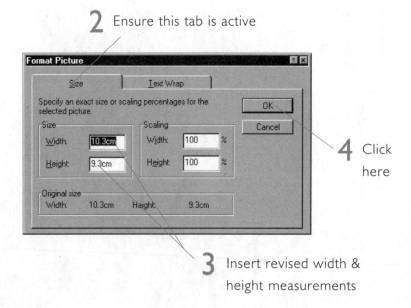

4 Click here

3 Insert revised width & height measurements

Bordering images

By default, the Word Processor does not apply a border to inserted pictures. However, you can apply a wide selection of borders if you want. You can specify:

* the border type

* the border thickness

* how many sides the border should have

* the border colour

* whether the bordered image should have a drop shadow

Applying a border

First, select the picture you want to border. Then pull down the Format menu and click Borders and Shading. Now do the following:

The Sample area displays a preview of what your border combination will look like.

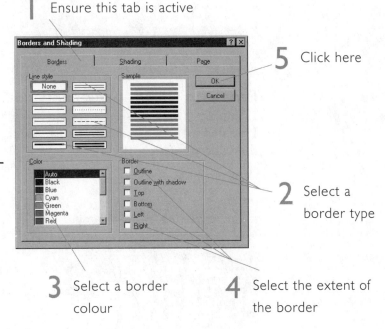

| Ensure this tab is active

5 Click here

2 Select a border type

3 Select a border colour

4 Select the extent of the border

Re step 4 – click Outline to have all 4 sides bordered. Or click Outline with shadow to impose a drop shadow, too. Then proceed as normal.

Moving images

You can easily move images from one location on the page to another.

First, click the image to select it. Move the mouse pointer over it; it changes to a pointing arrow. Left-click once and hold down the button. Drag the image to its new location (as you do so, the word 'MOVE' appears underneath the cursor).

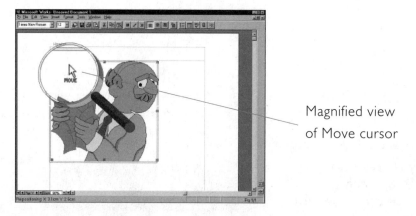

Magnified view of Move cursor

Release the mouse button to confirm the move.

Problems with Move operations?

If you find that dragging has no effect, select the image. Pull down the Format menu and click Picture. Carry out the following steps:

Ensure this tab is active

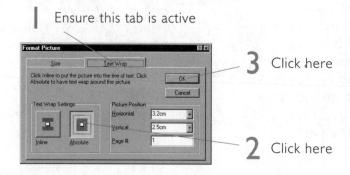

3 Click here

2 Click here

Now carry out the move again.

Page setup – an overview

You can control the following aspects of page layout in the Word Processor module:

- the top, bottom, left and/or right page margins

- the distance between the top page edge and the top edge of the header

- the distance between the bottom page edge and bottom edge of the footer

The illustration below shows these page components:

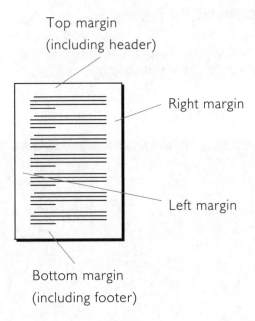

Top margin
(including header)

Right margin

Left margin

Bottom margin
(including footer)

You can also specify:

— the overall page size (inclusive of margins and headers/footers)

— the page orientation ('landscape' or 'portrait')

If none of the supplied page sizes is suitable, you can even customise your own.

Specifying margins

All documents have margins, because printing on the whole of a sheet is both unsightly and – in the case of many printers, since the mechanism has to grip the page – impossible. Documents need a certain amount of 'white space' (the unprinted portion of the page) to balance the areas which contain text and graphics. Without this, they can't be visually effective.

 Margin settings are the framework on which indents and tabs are based.

As a result, it's important to set margins correctly. Fortunately, the Word Processor module makes the job of changing margin settings easy.

Customising margins

Pull down the File menu and click Page Setup. Now carry out step 1 below. Then follow steps 2 or 3, as appropriate. Finally, carry out step 4:

I Ensure the Margins tab is active

4 Click here

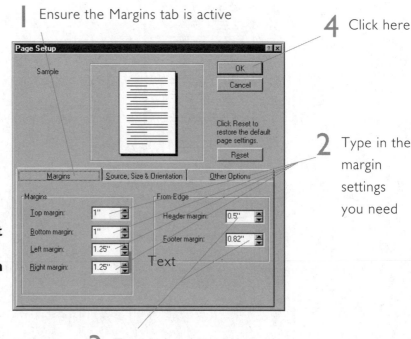

2 Type in the margin settings you need

 You can only adjust margin settings on a document-wide basis (not for individual pages).

3 Type in header and/or footer margin settings

Specifying the page size

The Word Processor comes with 11 preset page sizes. These are suitable for most purposes. However, if you need to you can also set up your own page definition.

There are two aspects to every page size:

- a vertical measurement

- a horizontal measurement

There are two possible orientations:

Portrait　　　　　　Landscape

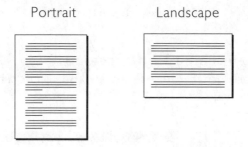

Setting the page size

Pull down the File menu and click Page Setup. Do the following:

Ensure this tab is active

To create your own page size, click Custom Size in step 2. Then type in the appropriate measurements in the Width & Height fields.

Finally, carry out step 4.

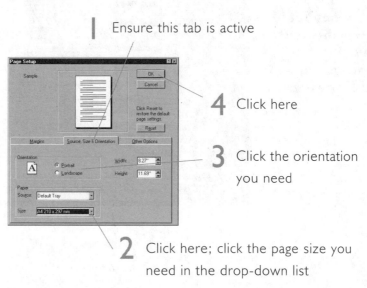

4 Click here

3 Click the orientation you need

2 Click here; click the page size you need in the drop-down list

Using Print Preview

The Word Processor provides a special view mode called Print Preview. This displays the active document exactly as it will look when printed.

Use Print Preview as a final check just before you print your document.

When you're using Print Preview, you can zoom in or out on the active page. What you can't do, however, is:

• display more than one page at a time

• edit or revise the active document (use Page Layout view instead)

Launching Print Preview
Pull down the File menu and click Print Preview. This is the result:

You can use a keyboard shortcut to leave Print Preview mode. Simply press Esc.

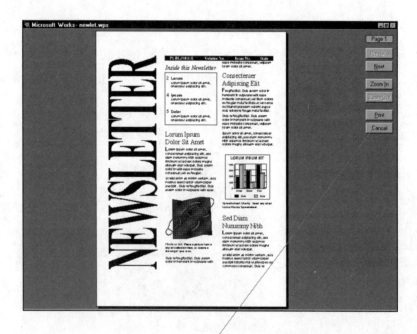

Click here to leave Print Preview and return to Normal or Page Layout view

Zooming in or out in Print Preview

There are two methods you can use here.

Using the mouse

Move the mouse pointer over the page area; it changes to a magnifying glass. Position this over the portion of the active document which you want to expand. Left-click once. Repeat this if necessary.

REMEMBER When you've reached the limit of magnification which Works supports, left-clicking with the mouse *decreases* the magnification.

A magnified view of part of the Print Preview screen

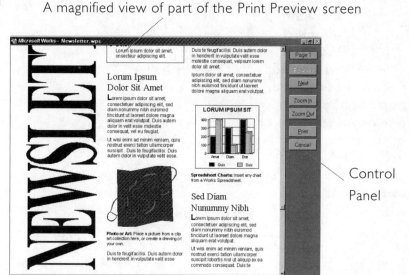

Control Panel

Using the Control Panel

Launch Print Preview. Then carry out the following actions:

REMEMBER Depending on the current level of magnification, one of the Zoom buttons may be greyed out, and therefore unavailable.

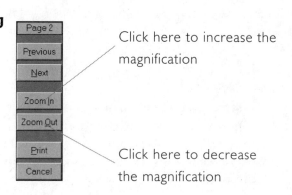

Click here to increase the magnification

Click here to decrease the magnification

Changing pages in Print Preview

Although you can only view one page at a time in Print Preview mode, you can step backwards and forwards through the document as often as necessary.

There are three methods you can use (in descending order of usefulness).

Using the Control Panel
Carry out the following actions:

 Depending on your location within the document (and the number of pages), one of these buttons may be greyed out, and therefore unavailable.

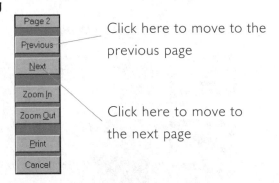

Click here to move to the previous page

Click here to move to the next page

Using the keyboard
You can use the following keyboard shortcuts:

 In a magnified page view, the Page Up and Page Down keys move through the current page.

Page Up	Moves to the previous page (unavailable within a magnified page view)
Page Down	Moves to the next page (unavailable within a magnified page view)
Up cursor	Within a magnified view of a page, moves towards the top of the page
Down cursor	Within a magnified view of a page, moves towards the base of the page

Using the scroll bars
When you're working with a magnified view of a page, use the vertical and/or horizontal scroll bars (using the standard Windows techniques) to move up or down within the page.

Printer setup

Most Word Processor documents need to be printed eventually. Before you can begin printing, however, you must ensure that:

The question of which printer you select affects how the document displays in Print Preview mode.

- the correct printer is selected (if you have more than one installed)

- the correct printer settings are in force

Works calls these collectively the 'printer setup'.

Irrespective of the printer selected, the settings vary in accordance with the job in hand. For example, most printer drivers (the software which 'drives' the printer) allow you to specify whether or not you want pictures printed. Additionally, they often allow you to specify the resolution or print quality of the output...

Selecting the printer and/or settings

Just before you're ready to print a document, pull down the File menu and click Print. Now do the following:

Re step 2 – for how to adjust printer settings, see your printer's manual.

Click here; select the printer you want from the list

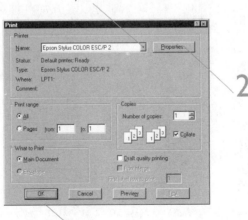

2 Click here to adjust the printer settings (then complete the dialog which launches)

Set any print options which are required *before* carrying out step 3 (see 'Customised Printing' on page 99 for how to do this).

3 Click here to begin printing

Printing – an overview

Once the active document is how you want it (and you've customised the printer setup appropriately), the next stage is to print it out. The Word Processor makes this process easy and straightforward. It lets you set a variety of options before you do so.

Alternatively, you can simply opt to print your document with the default options in force (the Word Processor provides a 'fast track' approach to this).

Available print options include:

- the number of copies you want printed

- whether you want the copies 'collated'. This is the process whereby Works prints one full copy at a time. For instance, if you're printing three copies of a 40-page document, Works prints pages 1-40 of the first document, followed by pages 1-40 of the second and pages 1-40 of the third.

- which pages you want printed

- the quality of the eventual output. With many printers, the Word Processor module allows you to print in Draft (with minimal formatting) for proofing purposes.
  This means that:

  - font styles (bold, italic, underline and strikethrough), pictures and colours don't print.

  - Works uses your default printer font (very often Courier or a variation on this) instead of the font you allocated.

  This option generally ensures that documents print more rapidly.

You can 'mix and match' these, as appropriate.

Customised printing

If you need to set revised print options before printing,
pull down the File menu and click Print. Now carry out
steps 1-4 below, as appropriate. To inspect your document
in Print Preview mode before printing, follow steps 5 and
6. Finally, carry out step 7.

5 Click here

4 Click here to print with
minimal formatting

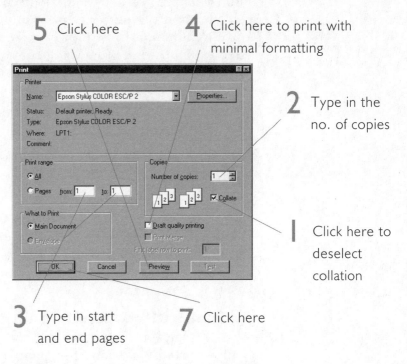

2 Type in the
no. of copies

1 Click here to
deselect
collation

3 Type in start
and end pages

7 Click here

 REMEMBER

After step 7, Works starts printing the active document.

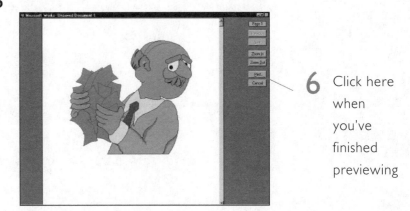

6 Click here
when
you've
finished
previewing

Printing – the fast track approach

Since documents and printing needs vary dramatically, it's often necessary to customise print options before you begin printing.

For example, if you've created a document which contains numerous pictures, you may well want to print out a draft copy for proofing purposes prior to printing the definitive version (although Print Preview mode provides a very effective indication of how a document will look when printed, there are still errors which are only detectable when you're working with hard copy). In this situation, you may wish to print in Draft mode (with minimal formatting).

For how to set your own print options, see the 'Customised printing' topic earlier.

On the other hand, simple documents can often benefit from a simple approach. In this case, you may well be content to print using the default options. Works recognises this and provides a method which bypasses the standard Print dialog, and is therefore much quicker and easier to use.

Printing with the current print options

First, ensure your printer is ready, and your document is ready to print. Make sure the Toolbar is visible. (If it isn't, pull down the View menu and click Toolbar).

Now do the following:

Click here

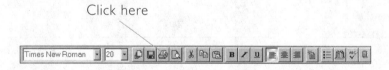

Works starts printing the active document immediately.

The Spreadsheet

This chapter gives you the basics of using the Spreadsheet module. You'll learn how to work with data and formulas, and how to move around in spreadsheets. You'll also discover how to locate data, and make it more visually effective. Finally, you'll customise page layout/printing.

Covers

Chapter Three

The Spreadsheet screen

Below is a detailed illustration of the Spreadsheet screen.

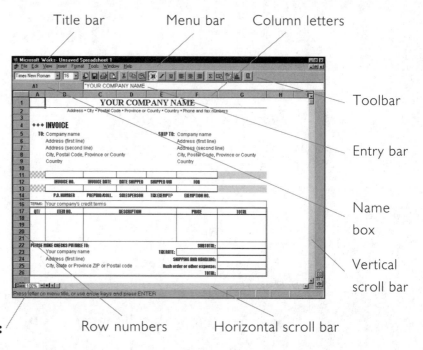

Title bar   Menu bar   Column letters

Toolbar

Entry bar

Name box

Vertical scroll bar

Row numbers   Horizontal scroll bar

REMEMBER

This is the Zoom area: The screen components here are used to adjust magnification levels. See the 'Changing Zoom levels' topic later.

Some of these – e.g. the scroll bars – are standard to just about all programs which run under Windows. One – the Toolbar – can be hidden, if required.

Specifying whether the Toolbar displays

Pull down the View menu. Then do the following:

REMEMBER

The ✔ signifies that the Toolbar is currently visible.

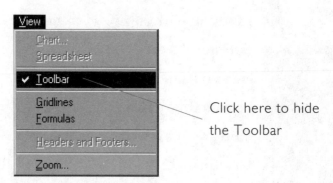

Click here to hide the Toolbar

Entering data

When you start the Works Spreadsheet module, you can use the Task Launcher to create a new blank spreadsheet (see Section 1 for how to do this). The result will look something like this:

Works applies the following names to new blank spreadsheets:
Spreadsheet 1
Spreadsheet 2
and so on...

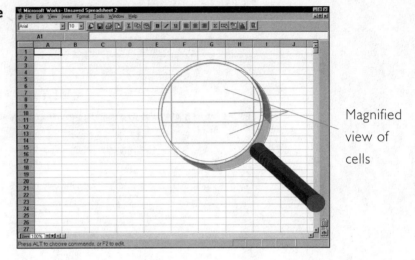

Magnified view of cells

Columns are vertical, rows horizontal. Each spreadsheet can have as many as 256 columns and 16,384 rows, making a grand total of 4,194,304 cells.

This means that you can start entering data immediately.

In the Spreadsheet module, you can enter the following basic data types:

- values (i.e. numbers)

- text (e.g. headings and explanatory material)

- functions (e.g. Sine or Cosine)

- formulas (combinations of values, text and functions)

You enter data into 'cells'. Cells are formed where rows and columns intersect. In the most basic sense, collections of rows/columns and cells are known as spreadsheets.

Although you can enter data *directly* into a cell (by simply clicking in it and typing it in), there's another method you can use which is often easier. The Spreadsheet provides a special screen component known as the Entry bar.

The illustration below shows the end of a blank spreadsheet. Some sample text has been inserted into cell IVl6384 (note that the Name box tells you which cell is currently active):

Name box

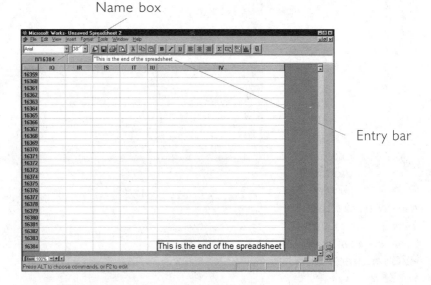

Entry bar

Entering data via the Entry bar

Click the cell you want to insert data into. Then click the Entry bar. Type in the data. Then follow step 1 below. If you decide not to proceed with the operation, follow step 2 instead:

You can use a keyboard route to confirm operations in the Entry bar. Simply press Return.

Click here

2 Click here to cancel the operation

Modifying existing data

HANDY TIP

You can spell-check spreadsheet contents. Press F7. Complete the Spelling dialog in line with the procedures on page 71.

You can amend the contents of a cell in two ways:

- via the Entry bar
- from within the cell

When you use either of these methods, the Spreadsheet enters a special state known as Edit Mode.

Amending existing data using the Entry bar

Click the cell whose contents you want to change. Then click in the Entry bar. Make the appropriate revisions and/or additions. Then press Return. The relevant cell is updated.

Amending existing data internally

HANDY TIP

You can 'freeze' row/ column titles so that they remain on screen when you move to other parts of the active spreadsheet. Select the row below the row you want to freeze, or the column to the right of the column you want to freeze. Pull down the Format menu and click Freeze Titles.

Click the cell whose contents you want to change. Press F2. Make the appropriate revisions and/or additions *within the cell*. Then press Return.

The illustration below shows a section of a spreadsheet created with the INVOICE TaskWizard.

A magnified view of cell C11, in Edit Mode

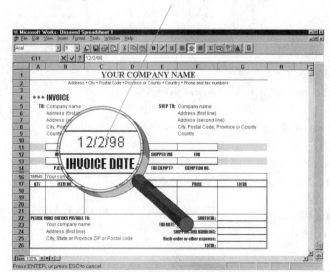

HANDY TIP

To unfreeze all frozen titles, pull down the Format menu and deselect Freeze Titles.

Working with cell ranges

To make the underlying structure of a spreadsheet's component cells more visible, pull down the View menu and click Gridlines.
   Repeat this procedure if you need to hide the structure.

Cells in a selected range are coloured black, with the exception of the first.

You can name ranges, for ease of use.
   Select the range. Pull down the Insert menu and click Range Name. In the Name field in the Range Name dialog, type in a name. Click OK.

When you're working with more than one cell, it's often convenient and useful to organise them in 'ranges'.

A range is a rectangular arrangement of cells. In the illustration below, cells B11, C11, D11, E11, F11, G11, B12, C12, D12, E12, F12 and G12 have been selected.

A selected cell range

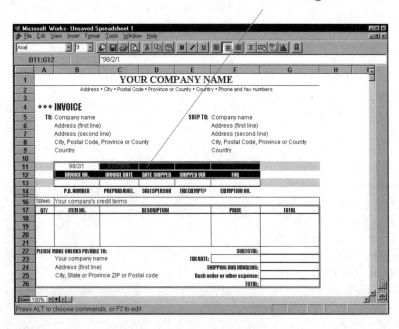

Cell 'shorthand'

The above description of the relevant cells is very cumbersome. It's much more useful to use a form of shorthand. The Spreadsheet module (using the start and end cells as reference points) refers to these cells as: $B_{11}:G_{12}$

This notation system makes it much easier to refer to sizeable cell ranges.

Moving around in spreadsheets

Spreadsheets can be huge. Moving to cells which happen currently to be visible is easy: you simply click in the relevant cell. However, the Spreadsheet module provides several techniques you can use to jump to less accessible areas.

Using the scroll bars

Use any of the following methods:

1. To scroll quickly to another section of the active spreadsheet, drag the scroll box along the scroll bar until you reach it

2. To move one window to the left or right, click to the left or right of the scroll box in the horizontal scroll bar

3. To move one window up or down, click above or below the scroll box in the vertical scroll bar

4. To move up or down by one row, click the arrows in the vertical scroll bar

5. To move left or right by one column, click the arrows in the horizontal scroll bar

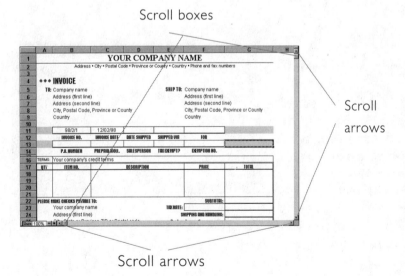

Scroll boxes

Scroll arrows

Scroll arrows

Using the keyboard
You can use the following techniques:

1. Use the cursor keys to move one cell left, right, up or down.

2. Hold down Ctrl as you use 1 above; this jumps to the edge of the current section (e.g. if cell B11 is active and you hold down Ctrl as you press →, Works jumps to IV11, the last cell in row 11).

3. Press Home to jump to the first cell in the active row, or Ctrl+Home to move to A1.

4. Press Page Up or Page Down to move up or down by one screen.

5. Press Ctrl+Page Down to move one screen to the right, or Ctrl+Page Up to move one screen to the left

You can use a keyboard shortcut to launch the Go To dialog
Simply press F5, or Ctrl+G.

Using the Go To dialog
The Spreadsheet provides a special dialog which you can use to specify precise cell destinations.

Pull down the Edit menu and click Go To. Now do the following:

Re step 1 – a cell's 'reference' (or 'address') identifies it in relation to its position in a spreadsheet, e.g. B11 **or** H23**.**
  You can also type in cell ranges here (e.g. B11:C15**), or range names.**

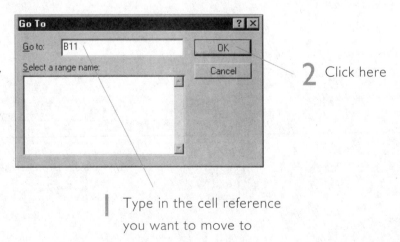

2 Click here

Type in the cell reference you want to move to

Changing Zoom levels

The ability to vary the level of magnification for the active document is especially useful for spreadsheets, which very often occupy more space than can be accommodated on-screen at any given time. Sometimes, it's helpful to 'zoom out' (i.e. decrease the magnification) so that you can take an overview; at other times, you'll need to 'zoom in' (increase the magnification) to work in greater detail.

You can alter magnification levels in the Spreadsheet module:

- with the use of the Zoom area

- with the Zoom dialog

Using the Zoom area

You can use the Zoom area (at the base of the screen) to alter zoom levels with the minimum of effort. Carry out step 1 OR 2, or steps 3 AND 4, as appropriate:

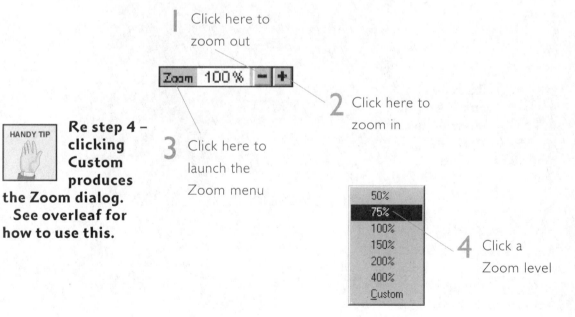

Click here to zoom out

Re step 4 – clicking Custom produces the Zoom dialog. See overleaf for how to use this.

HANDY TIP

2 Click here to zoom in

3 Click here to launch the Zoom menu

4 Click a Zoom level

Using the Zoom dialog

Using the Zoom dialog, you can perform either of the following:

- choose from preset zoom levels (e.g. 200%, 100%, 75%)

- specify your own zoom percentage

If you want to impose your own, custom zoom level, it's probably easier, quicker and more convenient to use the Zoom dialog.

Pull down the View menu and click Zoom. Now carry out step 1 or 2 below. Finally, follow step 3:

3 Click here

Re step 1 – entries must lie in the following range:
25%-1000%

Zoom

Zoom enlarges or shrinks the display to show more or less of your document. It does not affect printing.

OK

Cancel

Magnification (%)

- ○ 400
- ○ 200
- ○ 100
- ○ 75
- ○ 50
- ● Custom: 100

1 Type in your own zoom setting

2 Click a preset zoom level

Selection techniques

Before you can carry out any editing operations on cells in the Spreadsheet module, you have to select them first. Selecting a single cell is very easy: you merely click in it. However, there are a variety of selection techniques which you can use to select more than one cell simultaneously.

Selecting cell ranges with the mouse
The easiest way to select more than one cell at a time is to use the mouse.

Click in the first cell in the range; hold down the left mouse button and drag over the remaining cells. Release the mouse button.

Selecting cell ranges with the keyboard
There are two separate techniques you can use:

With the exception of the first cell, a selected range is filled with black.

- Position the cell pointer over the first cell in the range. Hold down one Shift key as you use the relevant cursor key to extend the selection. Release the keys when the correct selection has been defined

- Position the cell pointer over the first cell in the range. Press F8 to enter Selection mode. Use the cursor keys to define the selection area (see the illustration below). Finally, press F8 again to leave Selection mode

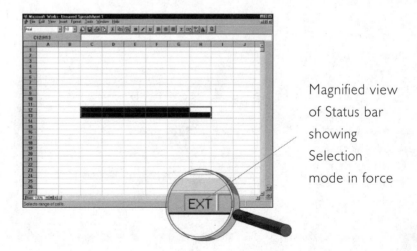

Magnified view of Status bar showing Selection mode in force

Selecting a single row or column

To select every cell within a row or column automatically, click the row or column heading.

Column heading

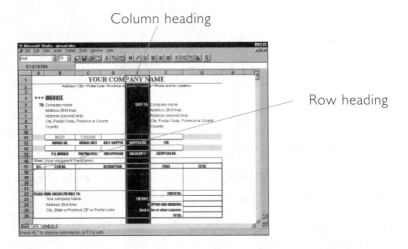

Row heading

Selecting multiple rows or columns

To select more than one row or column, click the row or column heading. Hold down the left mouse button and drag to select adjacent rows or columns.

Selecting an entire spreadsheet

Click the Select All button:

A magnified view of
the Select All button

HANDY TIP

You can use a keyboard shortcut to select every cell automatically. Simply press Ctrl+A, or Ctrl+Shift+F8.

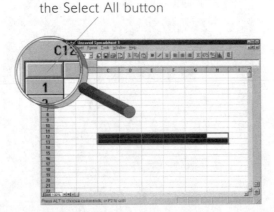

Formulas – an overview

Formulas are cell entries which define how other values relate to each other.

As a very simple example, consider the following:

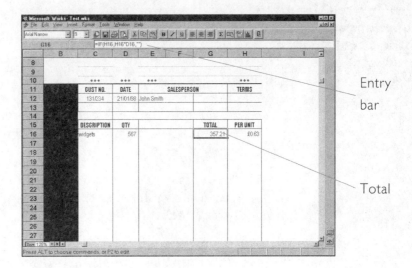

Cell G16 has been defined so that it multiplies the contents of cells D16 and H16. Obviously, in this instance you could insert the result easily enough yourself because the values are so small, and because we're only dealing with a small number of cells. But what happens if the cell values are larger and/or more numerous, or – more to the point – if they're liable to change frequently?

The answer is to insert a formula which carries out the necessary calculation automatically.

If you look at the Entry bar in the illustration, you'll see the formula which does this:

=IF(H16,H16*D16,"")

This is a fairly complex formula. Basically, it instructs Works to inspect cell H16. If an entry is found, the contents should be multiplied by the contents of D16, and the results displayed.

HANDY TIP

The H16*D16 **component tells Works to multiply the contents of the two cells. The** IF **before the bracket is the conditional operator.**

Inserting a formula

All formulas in the Spreadsheet begin with an equals sign. This is usually followed by a permutation of the following:

- an operand (cell reference, e.g. B4)

- a function (e.g. the summation function, SUM)

- an arithmetical operator (+, −, /, * and ^)

- comparison operators (=, <, >, <=, >= and <>)

The Spreadsheet supports a very wide range of functions organised into numerous categories. For more information on how to insert functions, see the 'Functions – an overview' topic.

The mathematical operators are (in the order in which they appear in the bulleted list): *plus, minus, divide, multiply* and *exponential*.

The comparison operators are (in the order in which they appear in the list): *equals, less than, greater than, less than or equal to, greater than or equal to* and *not equal to*.

There are two ways to enter formulas:

Entering a formula directly into the cell

Click the cell in which you want to insert a formula. Then type =, followed by your formula. When you've finished, press Return.

Entering a formula into the Entry bar

This is usually the most convenient method.

Click the cell in which you want to insert a formula. Then click in the Entry bar. Type =, followed by your formula. When you've finished, press Return or do the following:

Click here

G16   X ✓ ? =IF(H16,H16*D16,"")

Functions – an overview

Functions are pre-defined, built-in tools which accomplish specific tasks and then display the result. These tasks are very often calculations; occasionally, however, they're considerably more generalised (e.g. some functions simply return dates and/or times). In effect, functions replace one or more formulas.

The Spreadsheet module organises its functions under the following headings:

- Financial

- Date and Time

- Math and Trig

- Statistical

- Lookup and Ref

- Text

- Logical

- Informational

Works provides a special shortcut (called Easy Calc) which makes entering functions much easier and more straightforward. Easy Calc is very useful for the following reasons:

— It provides access to a large number of functions from a centralised source

— It ensures that functions are entered with the correct syntax

Functions can only be used in formulas. Note, however, that the result displays in the host cell, rather than the underlying function/formula.

 HANDY TIP

You can, however, have Works display formulas/ functions in situ within the spreadsheet.
  Simply pull down the View menu and click Formulas.

Using Easy Calc

Inserting a function with Easy Calc

At the relevant juncture during the process of inserting a formula, pull down the Tools menu and click Easy Calc. Now carry out step 1 OR 2 below:

If you follow step 2, Works launches the Insert Function dialog. Pick a function category in the Category field, then select the relevant function in the Choose a function box. Click Insert.

Now follow the instructions in the two remaining Easy Calc dialogs below.

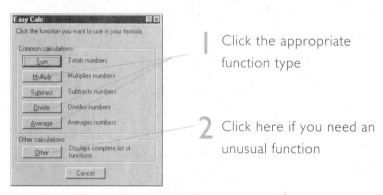

1 Click the appropriate function type

2 Click here if you need an unusual function

Now complete the following dialogs (the contents vary with the function selected):

Re step 3 – since we're inserting a Multiply function in this example, click the cells (within the spreadsheet itself) which you want multiplied (or define the appropriate cell range).

Works inserts the cell references and the relevant operator(s).

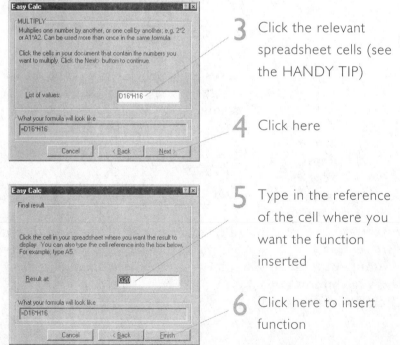

3 Click the relevant spreadsheet cells (see the HANDY TIP)

4 Click here

5 Type in the reference of the cell where you want the function inserted

6 Click here to insert function

Cell protection

Specific cells can be protected so that their contents are not overwritten. This is a two-stage process:

By default, all spreadsheet cells are locked, but not protected.

1. 'unlocking' those cells which you'll want to amend later (and therefore don't want to protect)

2. protecting the cells which are still locked (cell locking is ineffective until you do this)

You can also protect the active spreadsheet in its entirety.

Unlocking and protecting *specific* cells

Select the cells you *don't* want to protect. Pull down the Format menu and carry out steps 1, 2 and 4 below. Now (ensuring no cells are selected) pull down the Format menu again and carry out steps 1, 3 and 4 below:

| Click here

Re step 3 – Works protects those cells which have not been unlocked in the first stage in this operation.

2 Ensure this is deselected

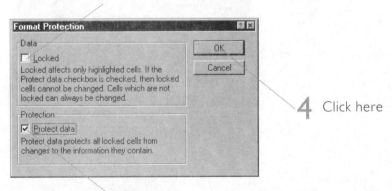

4 Click here

3 Ensure this is ticked

...contd

 The procedures here assume that no cells have been unlocked (see the 'Unlocking and protecting *specific* cells' section on page 117).

 If you want to remove cell protection, follow steps 1-2 again. (In step 1, however, ensure Protect data *isn't* ticked).

Protecting *all* cells in a spreadsheet

Pull down the Format menu and click Protection. Do the following:

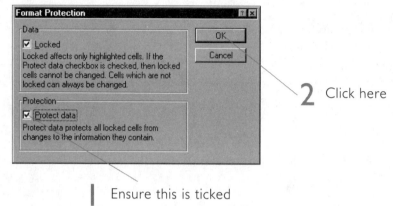

2 Click here

Ensure this is ticked

The effects of cell protection

When you've protected cells, the following results apply:

1. any attempt to overwrite/edit a locked cell produces a special message:

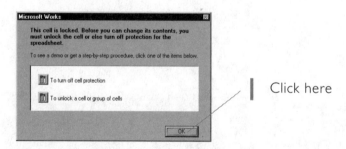

Click here

2. when a locked cell is selected, certain menu commands are greyed out

Amending row/column sizes

Sooner or later, you'll find it necessary to change the dimensions of rows or columns. This necessity arises when there is too much data in cells to display adequately. You can enlarge or shrink single or multiple rows/columns.

Changing row height

To change one row's height, click the row heading. If you want to change multiple rows, hold down Shift and click the appropriate extra headings. Then pull down the Format menu and click Row Height. Carry out the following steps:

2 Click here

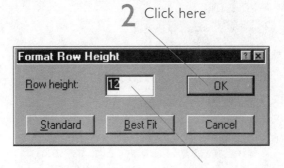

Type in the new height

 Works has a useful 'best fit' feature. Simply click Best Fit in either dialog to have the row(s) or column(s) adjust themselves automatically to their contents.

Changing column width

To change one column's width, click the column heading. If you want to change multiple columns, hold down Shift and click the appropriate extra headings. Then pull down the Format menu and click Column Width. Now do the following:

2 Click here

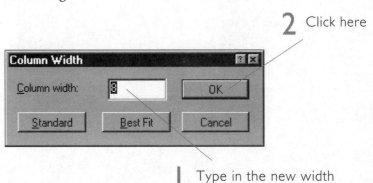

Type in the new width

Inserting rows or columns

You can insert additional rows or columns into spreadsheets.

Inserting a new row or column

First, select one or more cells within the row(s) or column(s) where you want to carry out the insert operation. Now pull down the Insert menu and carry out step 1 OR 2 below, as appropriate:

If you select cells in more than one row or column, Works inserts the equivalent number of new rows or columns.

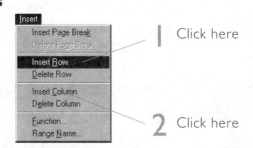

1 Click here

2 Click here

The new row(s) or column(s) are inserted immediately.

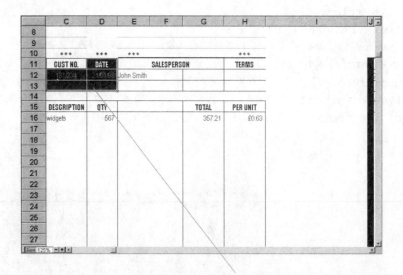

Here, two new columns or three new rows are being added

Working with fills

The Spreadsheet module lets you duplicate the contents of a selected cell down a column or across a row, easily and conveniently.

Use this technique to save time and effort.

Duplicating a cell
Click the cell whose contents you want to duplicate. Then move the mouse pointer over the appropriate border; the pointer changes to a cross and the word FILL appears.

REMEMBER

Here, cell A4 has been selected...

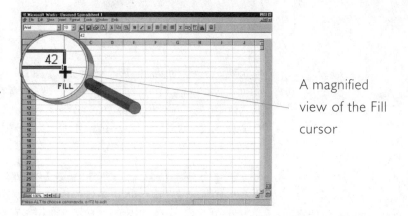

A magnified view of the Fill cursor

Click and hold down the button; drag the border over the cells into which you want the contents inserted. Release the button.

REMEMBER

The contents of A4 have been copied to A5:A20.

Using AutoFill

You can also carry out fills which *extrapolate* cell contents over the specified cells – Works calls these 'data series'. Look at the next illustration:

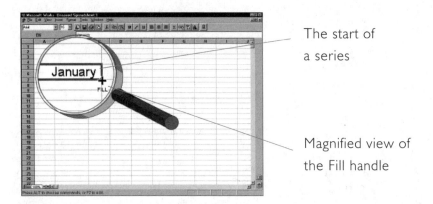

The start of a series

Magnified view of the Fill handle

If (as here) you wanted to insert month names in successive cells in a column, you could do so manually. But there's a much easier way. You can use AutoFill.

Using AutoFill to create a series

Type in the first element(s) of the series in consecutive cells. Select the cell(s). Then position the mouse pointer over the Fill handle in the bottom right-hand corner of the last cell (the pointer changes to a cross-hair). Hold down the left mouse button and drag the handle over the cells into which you want to extend the series. When you release the mouse button, Works extrapolates the initial entry or entries into the appropriate series.

In addition to months, data series can consist of:
- numbers (e.g. 1, 2, 3, 4 etc.)
- days of the week
- years
- alphanumeric combinations (e.g. Week 1, Week 2, Week 3 etc..)

The completed series

Working with headers

You can have the Spreadsheet print text at the top of each page within a document; the area of the page where repeated text appears is called the 'header'. In the same way, you can have text printed at the base of each page; in this case, the relevant page area is called the 'footer'. Headers and footers are printed within the top and bottom page margins, respectively.

To edit an *existing* header, simply follow the procedures outlined here; in step 1, amend the current header text as necessary.

Inserting a header

Pull down the View menu and click Headers and Footers. Now do the following:

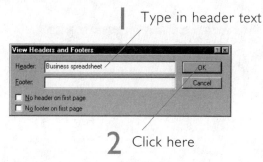

Type in header text

Click here

You can only view headers in Print Preview mode.

Viewing headers

Launch Print Preview mode – see page 144 for how to do this.

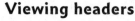

A header viewed in Print Preview

It isn't possible to amend the formatting of text in spreadsheet headers.

Working with footers

You can have the Spreadsheet automatically print text at the bottom of each page within a document; the area of the page where repeated text appears is called the 'footer'.

Footers are often used to display an abbreviated version of the spreadsheet's title.

To edit an *existing* footer, simply follow the procedures outlined here; in step 1, amend the current footer text as necessary.

Inserting a footer

Pull down the View menu and click Headers and Footers. Now do the following:

Type in footer text

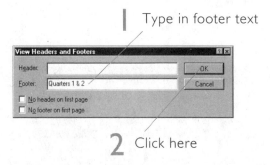

2 Click here

Viewing footers

Launch Print Preview mode – see page 144 for how to do this.

You can only view footers in Print Preview mode.

It isn't possible to amend the formatting of text in spreadsheet footers.

A footer viewed in Print Preview

Changing number formats

The Spreadsheet module lets you apply various formatting enhancements to cells and their contents. You can:

•   specify a number format

•   customise the font, type size and style of contents

•   specify cell alignment

•   border and/or shade cells

Specifying a number format

You can customise the way cell contents (e.g. numbers and dates/times) display. For example, you can specify at what point numbers are rounded up. Available formats are organised under several general categories. These include: Date, Percent and Fraction.

Select the cells whose contents you want to customise. Pull down the Format menu and click Number. Now do the following:

Ensure the Number tab is active

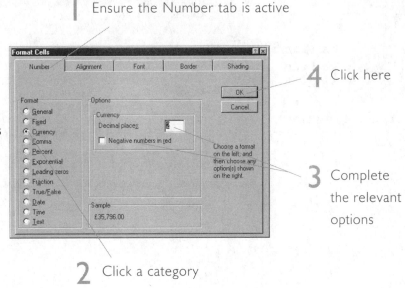

4 Click here

3 Complete the relevant options

2 Click a category

REMEMBER

Re step 3 – the options you can choose from vary according to the category chosen. Complete them as necessary.

Changing fonts and styles

The Spreadsheet module lets you carry out the following actions on cell contents (numbers, text or combinations of both):

- applying a new font

- applying a new type size

- applying a font style (*Italic*, **Bold**, <u>Underlining</u> or ~~Strikethrough~~)

- applying a colour

Amending the appearance of cell contents

Select the cell(s) whose contents you want to reformat. Pull down the Format menu and click Font and Style. Carry out step 1 below. Now follow any of steps 2-5, as appropriate. Finally, carry out step 6.

Ensure this tab is active

3 Type in a type size

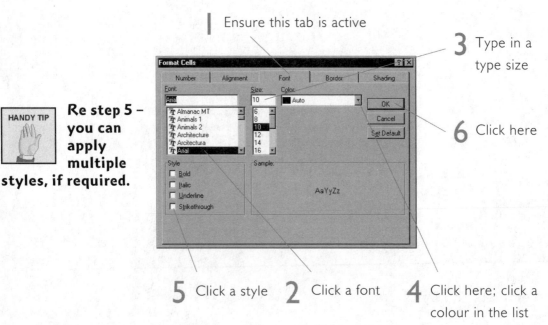

HANDY TIP

Re step 5 – you can apply multiple styles, if required.

6 Click here

5 Click a style **2** Click a font **4** Click here; click a colour in the list

Cell alignment

By default, Works aligns text to the left of cells, and numbers to the right. However, if you want you can change this.

You can specify alignment under two broad headings: Horizontal and Vertical.

Horizontal alignment
The main options are:

General	the default (see above)
Left	contents are aligned from the left
Right	contents are aligned from the right
Center	contents are centred
Fill	contents are duplicated so that they fill the cell
Center across selection	contents are centred across more than one cell (if you pre-selected a cell range)

Vertical alignment
Available options are:

Top	cell contents align with the top of the cell(s)
Center	contents are centred
Bottom	contents align with the cell bottom

Most of these settings parallel features found in the Word Processor module (and in many other word processors). The difference, however, lies in the fact that in spreadsheets Works has to align data within the bounds of cells rather than a page. When it aligns text, it often needs to employ its own version of text wrap. See overleaf for more information on this.

By default, when text is too large for the host cell, Works overflows the surplus into adjacent cells to the right. However, you can opt to have the Spreadsheet module force the text onto separate lines within the original cell. This process is called text wrap.

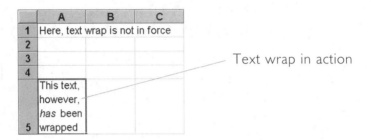

Text wrap in action

Customising cell alignment & applying text wrap

Select the relevant cell(s). Pull down the Format menu and click Alignment. Carry out step 1 below. Now follow any or all of steps 2-4, as appropriate. Finally, carry out step 5.

Ensure this tab is active

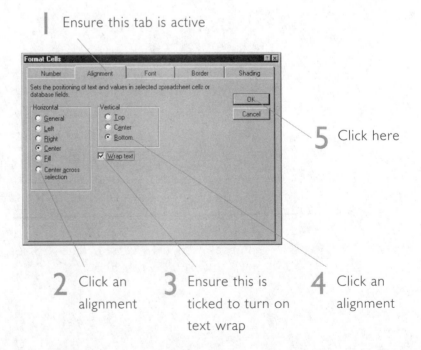

5 Click here

2 Click an alignment

3 Ensure this is ticked to turn on text wrap

4 Click an alignment

Bordering cells

Works lets you define a border around:

- the perimeter of a selected cell range

- the individual cells within a selected cell range

- specific sides within a cell range

You can customise the border by choosing from a selection of pre-defined border styles. You can also colour the border, if required.

Applying a cell border

First, select the cell range you want to border. Pull down the Format menu and click Border. Now carry out steps 1 and 2 below. Step 3 is optional. Finally, follow steps 4 and 5:

REMEMBER

If you're setting multiple border options, repeat steps 2-4 as required, *before* you carry out step 5.

HANDY TIP

Re step 4 – Outline borders the perimeter of the selected cells.
The other options (you can click more than 1) affect *individual* sides.

| Ensure this tab is active

2 Click a line style

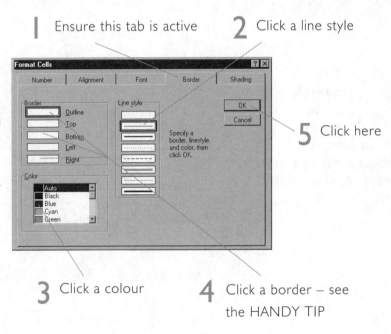

5 Click here

3 Click a colour

4 Click a border – see the HANDY TIP

Shading cells

Works lets you apply the following to cells:

- a pattern

- a pattern colour

- a background colour

You can do any of these singly, or in combination. Interesting effects can be achieved by using pattern colours with coloured backgrounds.

Applying a pattern or background

First, select the cell range you want to shade. Pull down the Format menu and click Shading. Now carry out step 1 below. Follow steps 2, 3 and/or 4 as appropriate. Finally, carry out step 5:

The Sample area previews how your background and pattern/colour will look.

1 Ensure this tab is active

5 Click here

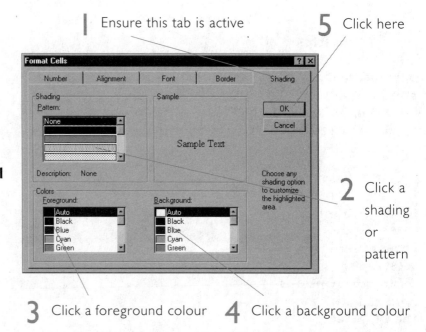

2 Click a shading or pattern

3 Click a foreground colour

4 Click a background colour

AutoFormat

Works provides a shortcut to the formatting of spreadsheet data: AutoFormat.

AutoFormat consists of 16 pre-defined formatting schemes. These incorporate specific excerpts from the font, number, alignment, border and shading options discussed earlier. You can apply any of these schemes (and their associated formatting) to selected cell ranges with just a few mouse clicks. Doing this saves a lot of time and effort, and the results are dependably professional.

AutoFormat works with most arrangements of spreadsheet data. However, if the effect you achieve isn't what you want, you can 'undo' it (providing you've carried out no intervening editing operations) by pressing Ctrl+Z.

Using AutoFormat

First, select the cell range you want to apply an automatic format to. Pull down the Format menu and click AutoFormat. Now carry out steps 1 and 2 below:

HANDY TIP **The Example field previews how your data will look with the specified AutoFormat.**

2 Click here

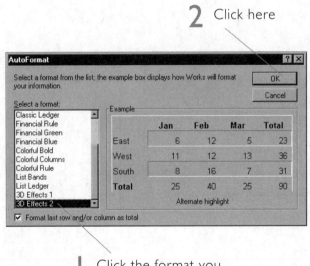

Click the format you want to apply

Find operations

The Spreadsheet lets you search for and jump to text and/or numbers (in short, any information) in your spreadsheets. This is a particularly useful feature when spreadsheets become large and complex, as they almost invariably do.

In Find operations, you can specify whether Works searches:

- by columns or rows

- in cells which contain formulas

- in cells which don't contain formulas

Searching for data

Place the mouse pointer at the location in the active spreadsheet from which you want the search to begin. Pull down the Edit menu and click Find. (Or press Ctrl+F). Now carry out step 1 below, then either of steps 2-3. Finally, carry out step 4:

If you want to restrict the search to specific cells, select a cell range *before* you follow steps 1-4.

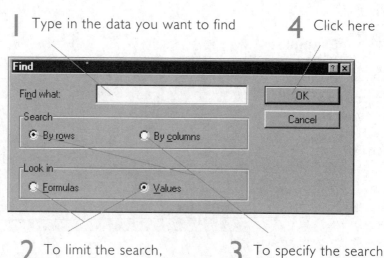

1 Type in the data you want to find

4 Click here

2 To limit the search, click the relevant option

3 To specify the search direction, click the relevant option

Search-and-replace operations

When you search for data, you can also – if you want – have Works replace it with something else.

Search-and-replace operations can be organised by rows or by columns. However, unlike straight searches, you can't specify whether Works looks in cells which contain formulas or those which don't.

Running a search-and-replace operation

Place the mouse pointer at the location in the active spreadsheet from which you want the search to begin. Pull down the Edit menu and click Replace. Carry out steps 1-3 below. Now do *one* of the following:

— Follow step 4. When Works locates the first search target, carry out step 5 to have it replaced. Repeat this process as often as necessary

— Carry out step 6 to have Works find every target and replace it automatically

1 Type in the data you want to find

4 Click here to find the 1st occurrence

5 Click here to replace it

HANDY TIP

If you want to restrict the search-and-replace operation to specific cells, select a cell range *before* you follow the procedures outlined here.

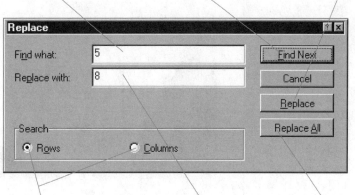

3 To specify the search direction, click the relevant option

2 Type in the replacement data

6 Click here to replace *all* occurrences

Charting – an overview

The Spreadsheet module has comprehensive charting capabilities. You can have it convert selected data into its visual equivalent. To do this, Works offers 12 chart formats:

- Area
- Bar
- Line
- Pie
- Stacked Line
- X-Y (Scatter)

- Radar
- Combination
- 3-D Area
- 3-D Bar
- 3-D Line
- 3-D Pie

When you create a chart, Works launches it in a separate Chart Editor window.
You can have as many as 8 charts associated with any spreadsheet.

Works uses a special dialog to make the process of creating charts as easy and convenient as possible.

The illustration below shows a sample 3-D Area chart:

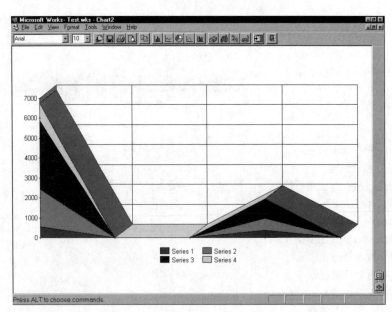

Creating a chart

HANDY TIP

When you select the data cells, include a row or column of text entries if you want these inserted into the chart as descriptive labels.

Select the cells you want to view as a chart. Pull down the Tools menu and click Create New Chart. Carry out steps 1-3 below. Follow steps 4-6 if you need to set advanced chart options. If you didn't follow steps 4-6, carry out step 7.

1 Ensure this tab is active

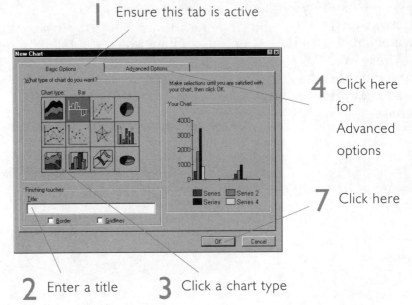

4 Click here for Advanced options

7 Click here

2 Enter a title

3 Click a chart type

5 Complete this section, as appropriate

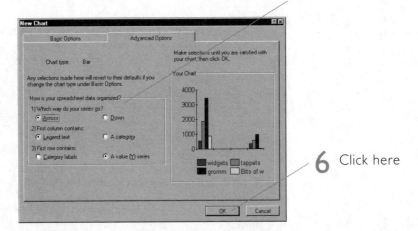

6 Click here

Amending chart formats

Once you've created a chart, you can easily change the underlying chart type. You can also apply a new sub-type.

Each basic chart type has several sub-types (variations) associated with it. These are unavailable when you first create your chart.

Switch to the chart whose format you want to change (if it isn't already open, first follow the procedure under 'Viewing charts' on page 138 to view it). Pull down the Format menu and click Chart Type. Now follow steps 1 and 2. If you want to apply a sub-type, carry out steps 3-5. If you *didn't* follow steps 3-5, follow step 6.

Ensure this tab is active

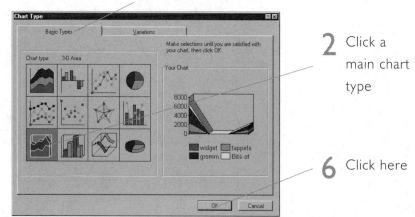

2 Click a main chart type

6 Click here

3 Click this tab

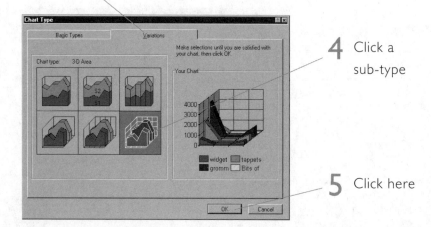

4 Click a sub-type

5 Click here

Reformatting charts

You can reformat charts in the following ways. You can:

- apply a new typeface/type size/font style to text

- apply a new colour/shade to graphic components

Text which is selected (like all chart objects) is surrounded by handles:

Reformatting text

Within the open chart, click the text you want to change. Pull down the Format menu and click Font and Style. Carry out any of steps 1-4, as appropriate. Finally, follow step 5:

2 Type in a type size

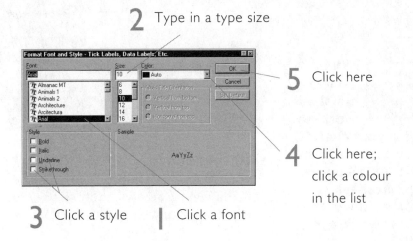

5 Click here

4 Click here; click a colour in the list

3 Click a style   1 Click a font

The series in a chart are the individual data entries.
  Below are sample series from a bar chart:

Reformatting graphic objects

Double-click the object (e.g. a series or pie slice) whose colour and/or shading you want to change. Now carry out step 1 and/or 2 below. Finally, follow step 3.

1 Click a colour

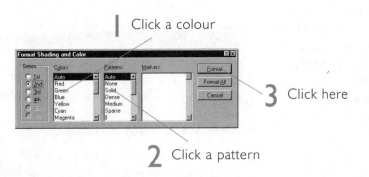

3 Click here

2 Click a pattern

Chart housekeeping

You can't select more than one chart at a time here.
To view multiple charts, simply repeat this procedure as often as required.

Viewing charts

A Works spreadsheet can have a maximum of 8 charts associated with it. To view a chart (when the spreadsheet or another chart is on-screen), pull down the View menu and click Chart. Now do the following:

Click the relevant chart

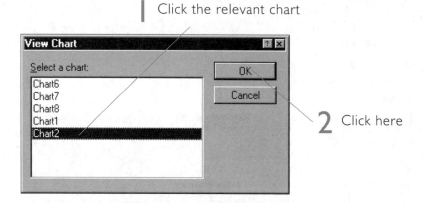

2 Click here

When you've finished working with your chart(s), you can return to the underlying spreadsheet by pulling down the View menu and clicking Spreadsheet.

Deleting charts

If you try to create more than 8 charts for a particular spreadsheet, Works will refuse to comply. The answer is to delete one or more earlier charts.

Switch to the chart you want to remove (or follow the procedure above to view it if it isn't already open). Pull down the Tools menu and click Delete Chart. Now do the following:

If you want to delete more than one chart, follow steps 1-2 as often as necessary.
Finally, carry out step 3.

Click the relevant chart

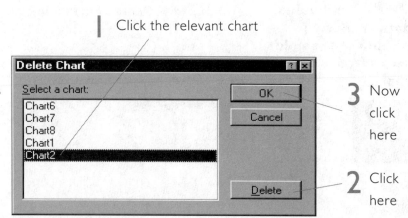

3 Now click here

2 Click here

Page setup – an overview

Making sure your spreadsheets print with the correct page setup can be a complex issue, for the simple reason that most become very extensive with the passage of time (so large, in fact, that in the normal course of things they won't fit onto a single page). Luckily, Works makes the entire page setup issue easy.

Page setup features you can customise include:

- the paper size

- the page orientation

- the starting page number

- margins

- whether gridlines are printed

- whether row and column headers are printed

Margin settings you can amend are:

— the top margin

— the bottom margin

— the left margin

— the right margin

Additionally, you can set the distance between the top page edge and the top of the header, and the distance between the bottom page edge and the bottom edge of the footer.

When you save your active spreadsheet, all Page Setup settings are automatically saved with it.

Setting size/orientation options

REMEMBER

Version 4 has fewer pre-defined paper types.

The Spreadsheet module comes with 17 pre-defined paper types which you can apply to your spreadsheets, in either portrait (top-to-bottom) or landscape (sideways on) orientation.

Portrait orientation

Landscape orientation

If none of the supplied page definitions is suitable, you can create your own.

Applying a new page size/orientation

Pull down the File menu and click Page Setup. Now carry out step 1 below, followed by steps 2-3 as appropriate. Finally, carry out step 4:

HANDY TIP

To create your own paper size, click Custom Size in step 2. Then type in the appropriate measurements in the Height & Width fields.

 Finally, carry out step 4.

Ensure this tab is active

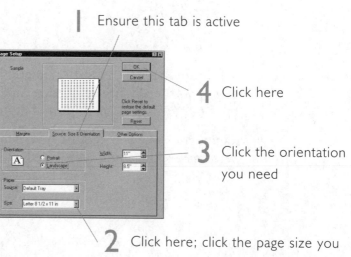

4 Click here

3 Click the orientation you need

2 Click here; click the page size you need in the drop-down list

Setting margin options

The Spreadsheet module lets you set a variety of margin settings. The illustration below shows the main ones:

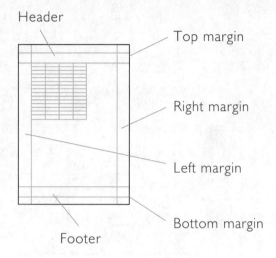

Header

Top margin

Right margin

Left margin

Bottom margin

Footer

Applying new margins

Pull down the File menu and click Page Setup. Now carry out step 1 below, followed by steps 2-3 as appropriate. Finally, carry out step 4:

Ensure this tab is active

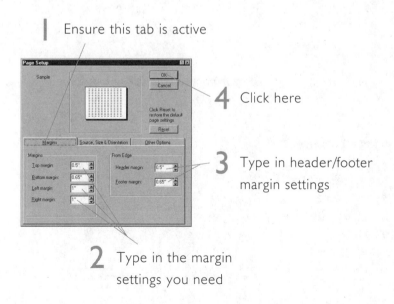

4 Click here

3 Type in header/footer margin settings

2 Type in the margin settings you need

Other page setup options

You can determine whether gridlines and row/column headings print. These are demonstrated below:

Column heading

This is an excerpt from the Print Preview screen.
For how to use **Print Preview** in the **Spreadsheet, see page 144.**

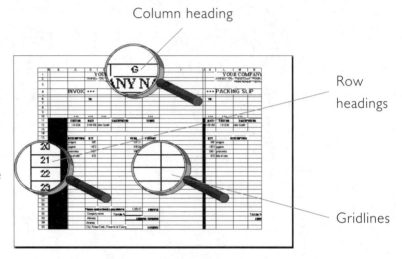

Row headings

Gridlines

Printing gridlines and row/column headings

Pull down the File menu and click Page Setup. Now carry out step 1 below, followed by steps 2-3 as appropriate. Finally, carry out step 4:

Ensure this tab is active

4 Click here

Re step 2 – here, you can set the page number for the first page in your spreadsheet – the default is: '1'.

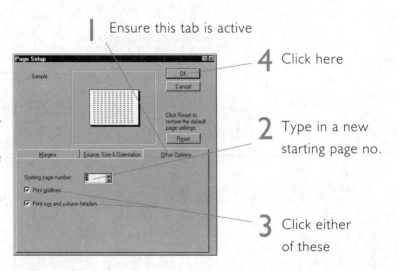

2 Type in a new starting page no.

3 Click either of these

Page setup for charts

Most page setup issues for charts are identical to those for spreadsheet data. However, there are differences. The following additional options are available:

Full page	the chart is expanded to fill the page, with its width/height ratio disrupted, if necessary
Full page, keep proportions	the chart is scaled to fit the page, but with its width/height ratio unaltered
Screen size	the chart is reduced to the size of your computer screen (so that it occupies roughly 25% of the page)

Customising printed chart sizes

Pull down the File menu and click Page Setup. Now carry out steps 1-3 below:

Ensure this tab is active

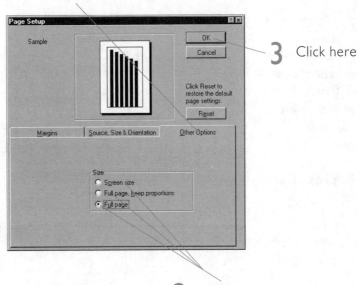

3 Click here

2 Click any scale option

Using Print Preview

The Spreadsheet module provides a special view mode called Print Preview. This displays the active spreadsheet (one page at a time) exactly as it will look when printed. Use Print Preview as a final check just before you begin printing.

When you're using Print Preview, you can zoom in or out on the active page. What you can't do, however, is:

- display more than one page at a time

- edit or revise the active document

Launching Print Preview

Pull down the File menu and click Print Preview. This is the result:

A preview of a chart

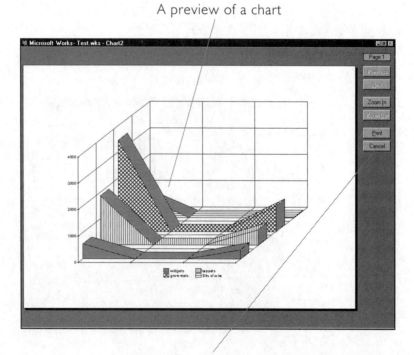

REMEMBER

**You can use a keyboard shortcut to leave Print Preview mode and return to your spreadsheet or chart.
Simply press Esc.**

Click here to leave Print Preview and return to Normal or Page Layout view

Zooming in or out in Print Preview

There are two methods you can use here.

Using the mouse

Move the mouse pointer over the page area; it changes to a magnifying glass. Position this over the portion of the active spreadsheet or chart which you want to expand. Left-click once. Repeat this if necessary.

REMEMBER

When you've reached the limit of magnification which Works supports, left-clicking with the mouse *decreases* the magnification.

A magnified view of part of the Print Preview screen

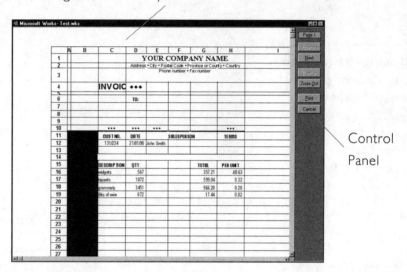

Control Panel

Using the Control Panel

Launch Print Preview. Then carry out the following actions:

HANDY TIP

Depending on the current level of magnification, one of the Zoom buttons may be greyed out, and therefore unavailable.

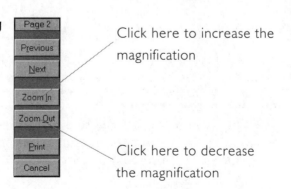

Click here to increase the magnification

Click here to decrease the magnification

Changing pages in Print Preview

Although you can only view one page at a time in Print Preview mode, you can step backwards and forwards through the spreadsheet as often as necessary.

There are three methods you can use (in descending order of usefulness).

Using the Control Panel
Carry out the following actions:

Depending on your location within the document (and the number of pages), one of these buttons may be greyed out, and therefore unavailable.

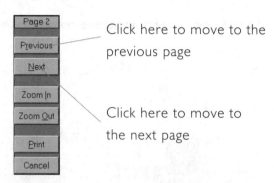

Click here to move to the previous page

Click here to move to the next page

Using the keyboard
You can use the following keyboard shortcuts:

In a magnified page view, the Page Up and Page Down keys move through the current page.

Page Up	Moves to the previous page (unavailable within a magnified page view)
Page Down	Moves to the next page (unavailable within a magnified page view)
Up cursor	Within a magnified view of a page, moves towards the top of the page
Down cursor	Within a magnified view of a page, moves towards the base of the page

Using the scroll bars
When you're working with a magnified view of a page, use the vertical and/or horizontal scroll bars (using standard Windows techniques) to move up or down within the page.

Printing spreadsheet data

When you print your data, you can specify:

• the number of copies you want printed

• whether you want the copies 'collated'. This is the process whereby Works prints one full copy at a time. For instance, if you're printing five copies of a 12-page spreadsheet, Works prints pages 1-12 of the first copy, followed by pages 1-12 of the second and pages 1-12 of the third... and so on.

• which pages you want printed

• the printer you want to use (if you have more than one installed on your system)

You can 'mix and match' these, as appropriate.

Starting a print run

Open the spreadsheet which contains the data you want to print. Then pull down the File menu and click Print. Do any of steps 1-4. Then carry out step 5 to begin printing:

If you need to adjust your printer's internal settings before you initiate printing, click Properties. Then refer to your printer's manual.

Click Draft quality printing to have your spreadsheet print with minimal formatting.

1 Click here; select a printer from the list

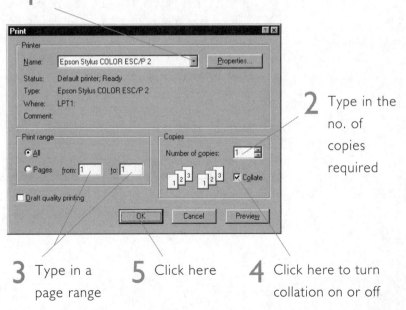

2 Type in the no. of copies required

3 Type in a page range

5 Click here

4 Click here to turn collation on or off

Printing – the fast track approach

In earlier topics, we've looked at how to customise print options to meet varying needs and spreadsheet sizes. However, the Spreadsheet module – like the Word Processor – recognises that there will be times when you won't need this level of complexity. There are occasions when you'll merely want to print out your work – often for proofing purposes – with the standard print defaults applying.

These are:

- Works prints only the active spreadsheet

- Works prints only 1 copy

- Works prints all pages within the active spreadsheet

- collation is turned off

- Works prints with full (not Draft) formatting

For this reason, Works provides a method which bypasses the standard Print dialog, and is therefore much quicker and easier to use.

Printing with the default print options

First, open the spreadsheet you want to print. Ensure your printer is ready. Make sure the Toolbar is visible. (If it isn't, pull down the View menu and click Toolbar). Now do the following:

Click here

Works starts printing data in the active spreadsheet immediately.

The Database

This chapter gives you the basics of using the Database. You'll learn how to work with data and formulas, and how to move around in databases. You'll also discover how to locate data, and apply formatting to make it more visually effective. Finally, you'll customise page layout/printing.

Chapter Four

Covers

The Database screen

Below is a detailed illustration of a typical Database screen.

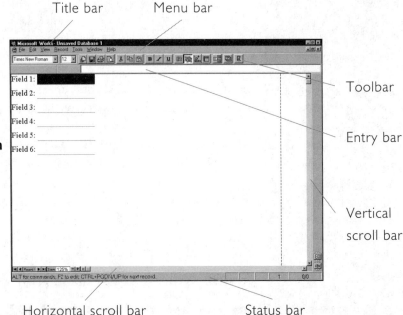

Title bar   Menu bar

Toolbar

Entry bar

Vertical scroll bar

Horizontal scroll bar   Status bar

REMEMBER

This is Form view. For more information on Database views, see the 'Using Database views' topic later.

Some of these – e.g. the rulers and scroll bars – are standard to just about all programs which run under Windows. One – the Toolbar – can be hidden, if required.

Specifying whether the Toolbar displays

Pull down the View menu and do the following:

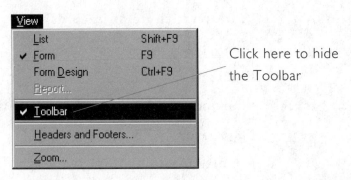

Click here to hide the Toolbar

REMEMBER

The ✔ signifies that the Toolbar is currently visible.

Creating your first database

REMEMBER **See the 'Creating blank documents'** topic in Section 1 for how to use the Task Launcher to create a new Database document.

Unlike the Word Processor and Spreadsheet modules, the Database *doesn't* create a new blank document immediately after you've launched the module from within the Task Launcher. Instead, you have to complete several dialogs first. Do the following:

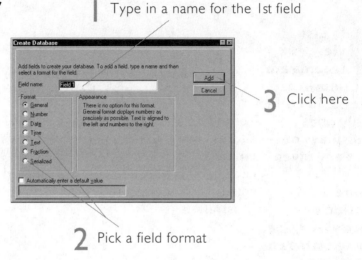

Type in a name for the 1st field

3 Click here

2 Pick a field format

REMEMBER **Database fields are single columns of** information (in List view) or spaces for the insertion of information (in Form view).

After you've followed step 3, Works reproduces the same dialog so that you can create the second field. Repeat the above procedures as often as necessary. When you've defined your final field, do the following:

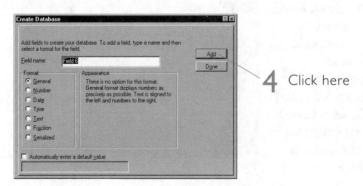

4 Click here

Entering data

When you've created a database, you can begin entering data immediately. You can enter the following basic data types:

- numbers

- text

- functions

- formulas (combinations of numbers, text and functions)

You enter data into 'fields'. Fields are organised into 'records'. Records are whole units of related information.

To understand this, we'll take a specific example. In an address book, the categories under which information is entered (e.g. Surname, Address, Phone No.) are fields, while each person whose details are entered into the database constitutes one record. This is shown in the next illustration:

In List view, records are shown as single rows. In Form view, only one record displays on-screen at any given time.

For more information on Database views, see the 'Using Database views' topic on page 155 - 156.

This is List view. List view is suitable for the mass insertion of data (more than 1 record is visible at a time). However, you can also enter data in Form view.

Fields

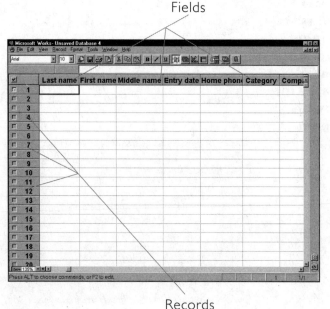

Records

...contd

Although you can enter data *directly* into a database field (by simply clicking in it and typing it in), there's another method you can use which is often easier. Like the Spreadsheet module, the Database provides a special screen component known as the Entry bar.

In the illustration below, two fields in the first record have been completed.

Entry bar

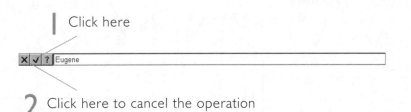

Entering data via the Entry bar

Click the field you want to insert data into. Then click the Entry bar. Type in the data. Then follow step 1 below. If you decide not to proceed with the operation, follow step 2 instead:

You can use a keyboard route to confirm operations in the Entry bar. Simply press Return.

| Click here

X ✓ ? Eugene

2 Click here to cancel the operation

Modifying existing data

You can amend the contents of a field in two ways:

- via the Entry bar

- from within the field itself

When you use either of these methods, the Database enters a special state known as Edit Mode.

Amending existing data using the Entry bar

Click the field whose contents you want to change. Then click in the Entry bar. Make the appropriate revisions and/or additions. Then press Return. The relevant field is updated.

Amending existing data internally

Click the field whose contents you want to change. Press F2. Make the appropriate revisions and/or additions *within the field*. Then press Return.

The illustration below shows our new database, in Form view.

This is the first record in our database.

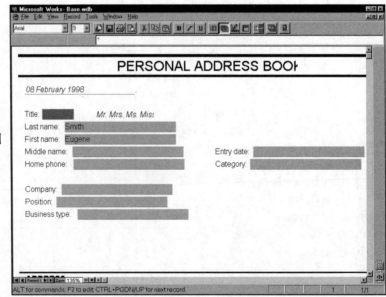

Using Database views

The Database module provides two principal views:

List

List view presents your data in a grid structure reminiscent of the Spreadsheet module, with the columns denoting fields and the rows individual records. Pictures and most formatting components do not display.

Use List view for bulk data entry or comparison.

Form

Form view limits the display to one record at a time, while presenting it in a way which is more visual and therefore easier on the eye. The basis of this view is the 'form', the underlying database layout which you can customise in Form Design view. Pictures and formatting display in Form view (although you can only initiate or modify them in Form Design view).

In many circumstances, Form view provides the best way to interact with your database.

 REMEMBER

Form Design view is a subset of Form view.

A database in Form view...

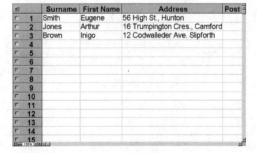

And in List view

...contd

You can use three methods to switch to another view.

The menu approach...

Pull down the View menu and do the following:

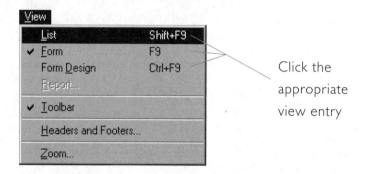

Click the appropriate view entry

The Toolbar approach...

Make sure the Toolbar is visible. (If it isn't, pull down the View menu and click Toolbar). Now click one of the following:

List view   Form Design view

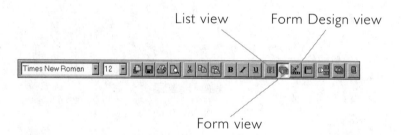

Form view

The keyboard approach...

Use any of the following combinations:

F9	Form view
Shift+F9	List view
Ctrl+F9	Form Design view

Moving around in databases

Databases can quickly become very large. The Database module provides several techniques you can use to find your way round.

Using the scroll bars
Use any of the following methods:

1. To scroll quickly to another record (in List view) or to another field (in Form view), drag the scroll box along the scroll bar until you reach it

2. To move one window to the right or left, click to the left or right of the scroll box in the Horizontal scroll bar

3. To move one window up or down, click above or below the scroll box in the Vertical scroll bar

4. To move up or down by one record (in List view) or one field (in Form view), click the arrows in the Vertical scroll bar

5. To move left or right by one field, click the arrows in the Horizontal scroll bar

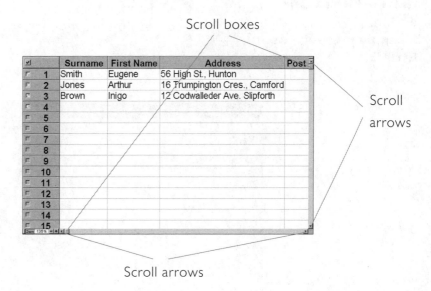

Scroll boxes

Scroll arrows

Scroll arrows

...contd

Using the keyboard
You can use the following techniques:

1. In List view, use the cursor keys to move one field left, right, up or down. In Form view, use the up and left cursor keys to move one field up, or the down and right keys to move one field down

2. Press Home to jump to the first field in the active record, or End to move to the last

3. Press Ctrl+Home to move to the first record in the open database, or Ctrl+End to move to the last

4. Press Page Up or Page Down to move up or down by one screen

5. In Form view, press Ctrl+Page Down to move to the next record, or Ctrl+Page Up to move to the previous one

HANDY TIP **You can use a keyboard shortcut to launch the Go To dialog.**
  Simply press F5, or Ctrl+G.

Using the Go To dialog
The Database provides a special dialog which you can use to specify precise field or record destinations.

Pull down the Edit menu and click Go To. Now carry out step 1 OR 2 below. Finally, follow step 3.

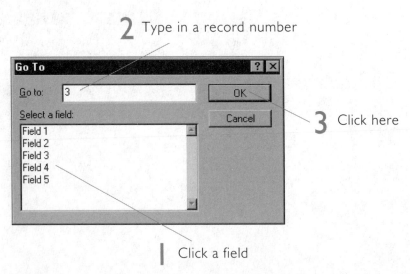

2 Type in a record number

3 Click here

Click a field

Using Zoom

The ability to vary the level of magnification in the Database module is very useful. Sometimes, it's helpful to 'zoom out' (i.e. decrease the magnification) so that you can take an overview; at other times, you'll need to 'zoom in' (increase the magnification) to work in greater detail. Works makes this process easy and convenient.

You can change magnification levels in the Database module:

• with the use of the Zoom area

• with the Zoom dialog

Using the Zoom area

You can use the Zoom area (at the base of the screen) to alter zoom levels with the minimum of effort. Carry out step 1 or 2, or steps 3-4, as appropriate:

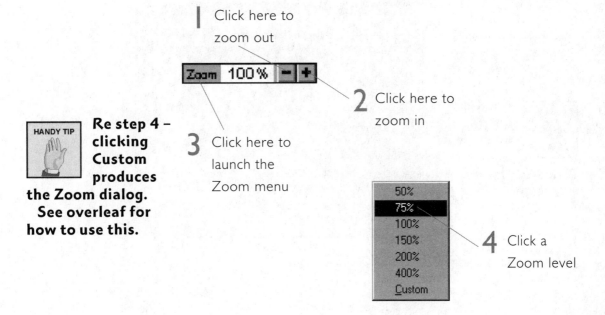

1 Click here to zoom out

2 Click here to zoom in

3 Click here to launch the Zoom menu

4 Click a Zoom level

Re step 4 – clicking Custom produces the Zoom dialog. See overleaf for how to use this.

Using the Zoom dialog

Using the Zoom dialog, you can perform either of the following operations:

- choosing from preset zoom levels (e.g. 200%, 100%, 75%)

- specifying your own zoom percentage

If you want to impose your own, custom zoom level, it's probably easier, quicker and more convenient to use the Zoom dialog.

Pull down the View menu and click Zoom. Now carry out step 1 or 2 below. Finally, follow step 3:

3 Click here

BEWARE

Re step 1 – entries must lie in the following range: 25%-1000%

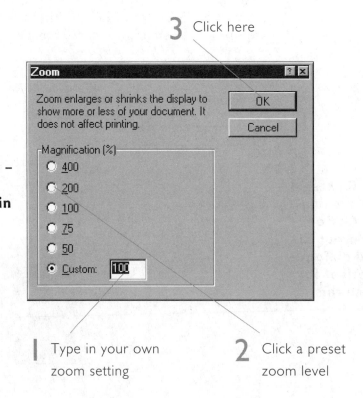

1 Type in your own zoom setting

2 Click a preset zoom level

Selection techniques in List view

Before you can carry out any editing operations on fields or records in the Database module, you have to select them first. The available selection techniques vary according to whether you're currently using List, Form or Form Design view.

In List view, follow any of the techniques below:

Using the mouse

To select a single field	Simply click in it
To select multiple fields	Click the field in the top left-hand corner; hold down the mouse button and drag over the fields you want to highlight. Release the mouse button
To select one record	Click the record number
To select multiple records	Hold down Shift as you click the record numbers

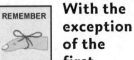

REMEMBER

With the exception of the first, selected fields are filled with black.

☑		Surname	First Name	Address	Post Code	Phone No.
☐	1	Smith	Eugene	56 High St., Hunton		
☐	2	Jones	Arthur	16 Trumpin Camford		
☐	3	Brown	Inigo	12 Codwalleder Ave. Slipforth		

Record numbers

Using the keyboard

HANDY TIP

To select the whole of the active database in List view, press Ctrl+Shift+F8.

To select multiple fields	Position the insertion point in the first field. Press F8. Use the cursor keys to extend the selection area. Press F8 when you've finished
To select a whole record	Position the insertion point in the record. Press Ctrl+F8
To select a whole field	Position the insertion point in the field. Press Shift+F8

Selection techniques in forms

Note that some of the techniques discussed here **(they're clearly marked) will only work in Form Design view.**

Using the mouse

To select a single field — Simply click in it.

To select multiple fields — Hold down Ctrl as you click in successive fields (you must be in Form Design view to do this).

To select one record — Do any of the following:

To previous record   To final record

To first record   To next record

These arrow buttons can be found in the bottom left-hand corner of the Form view screen.

To select multiple field names or inserted pictures — In Form Design view, hold down Ctrl as you click successive objects.

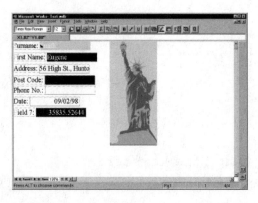

Several fields (and an image) selected in Form Design view

Using the keyboard

To select a field — Use the cursor keys to position the insertion point in the relevant field

To select a record — Press Ctrl+Page Up or Ctrl+Page Down until the record you want is displayed

Formulas – an overview

You can insert formulas into Database fields. Formulas in the Database module work in much the same way as in the Spreadsheet. However, there are fewer applications for them.

Database formulas serve two principal functions:

- to ensure that the same entry appears in a given field throughout every record in a database

- to return a value based on the contents of multiple additional fields

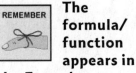

The formula/ function appears in the Entry bar:

Look at the next illustration:

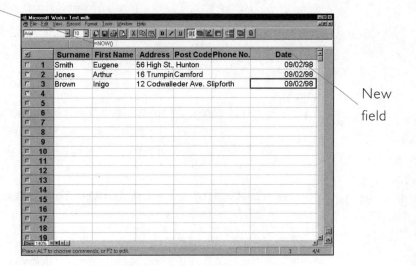

New field

Here, an extra field has been added (see later for how to do this) and a formula (in this case, consisting entirely of a function) inserted. The function:

=NOW()

inserts the current system date in the Date field within every record.

Inserting a formula

As in the Spreadsheet module, all Database formulas must begin with an equals sign. This is usually followed by a permutation of the following:

Arguments (e.g. field references) relating to functions are always contained in brackets.

- one or more operands (in the case of the Database module, field names)

- a function (e.g. AVG – returns the Average)

- an arithmetical operator (+, –, /, * and ^)

The Database supports a very wide assortment of functions. For more information on how to insert functions, refer to page 166.

The arithmetical operators are (in the order in which they appear in the bulleted list above):

plus, *minus*, *divide*, *multiply* and *exponential*.

There are two ways to enter formulas:

Entering a formula directly into the field

Click the field into which you want to insert a formula. Then type =, followed by your formula. When you've finished defining the formula, press Return.

Entering a formula into the Entry bar

This is usually the most convenient method.

Click the field in which you want to insert a formula. Then click in the Entry bar. Type =, followed by your formula. When you've finished defining the formula, press Return or do the following:

Click here

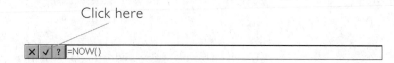

Database functions

In many ways, the Database module's implementation of functions parallels that of the Spreadsheet module. However, there is one important difference: you can't use Easy Calc to insert them. Instead, you have to do so manually. Luckily, though, the inbuilt HELP system provides assistance.

Using HELP before you insert a function

Pull down the Help menu and click Contents. Now do the following:

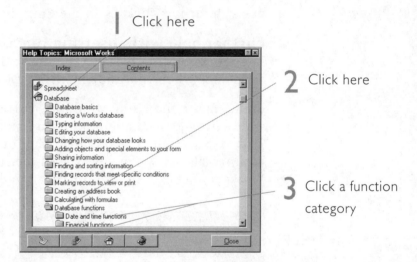

Click here

2 Click here

3 Click a function category

After you've followed step 4, Works launches a HELP window with function-specific assistance.
  To close the window when you've finished with it, click this button:

Shrink Help

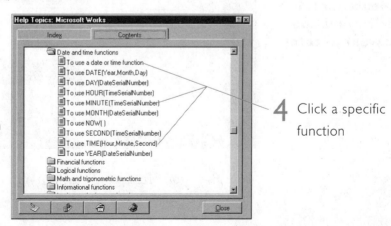

4 Click a specific function

Inserting a function

There are two ways to insert functions:

See 'Further help with inserting functions' below for how to complete function arguments.

Entering a function directly into the field

Click the field into which you want to insert the function. Type = followed by the function itself. Finally, press Return to confirm the operation.

Entering a function into the Entry bar

Click the field in which you want to insert the function. Then click in the Entry bar. Type = followed by your function. When you've finished defining the function, press Return or click ✓ in the Entry bar.

Further help with inserting functions

The Works on-line HELP system provides additional assistance when you implement functions.

First, ensure the HELP window is currently displayed. (If it isn't, click 🔲 in the bottom right-hand corner of the Database screen). Then follow either of the procedures outlined above. When you type in the function name, Works launches a special function window:

The HELP window provides syntax guidance for the specific function you want to enter.

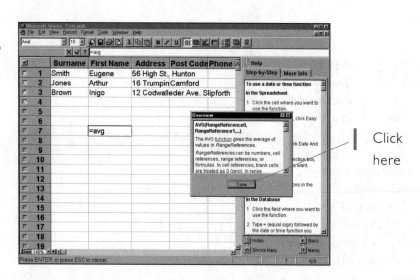

Click here

Complete your function's arguments in the normal way, then follow step 1 above.

Inserting fields

You can add one or more blank fields to the active database, from either Form Design (but not Form) or List view.

Adding a field in Form Design view

If you're not already in Form Design view, pull down the View menu and click Form Design. Click where you want the new field inserted. Pull down the Insert menu and click Field. Do the following:

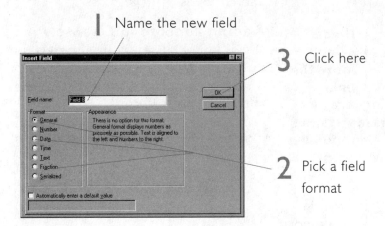

Name the new field

3 Click here

2 Pick a field format

Adding one or more fields in List view

If you're not currently in List view, pull down the View menu and click List. Click in the field next to which you want the new field(s) added. Pull down the Record menu and click Insert Field. In the sub-menu, click Before or After, as appropriate.

The Insert Field dialog launches. Follow steps 1-2 above, then click the Add button. The dialog now changes. Do *either* of the following:

HANDY TIP

Repeat ß as often as necessary to add as many additional fields as required.

A.   Click Done to add the single field and close the dialog.

B.   Carry out steps 1-2 again (then click Add) to add a further field.

If you carried out B, click Done when you've added the correct number of new fields.

Inserting records

See the 'Moving around in databases' topic earlier for how to jump to the relevant record.

You can add one or more blank records to the active database, from within either Form (but not Form Design) or List view.

Adding a record in Form view

If you're not already in Form view, pull down the View menu and click Form. Go to the record before which you want the new record to appear. Pull down the Record menu and click Insert Record.

Adding a record in List view

If you select more than one existing record, Works inserts the equivalent number of new records.

If you're not currently in List view, pull down the View menu and click List. Click in the record above which you want the new record added. Pull down the Record menu and click Insert Record.

To hide one record in Form view, go to it. In List view, however, select one or more records. Now in either case pull down the Record menu and click Hide Record.
    To make all records visible again, pull down the Record menu and click Show All Records.

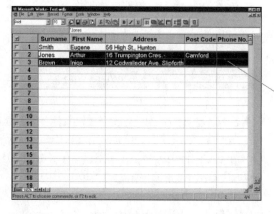

Preparing to add two new records in List view...

The records have been added

Amending record/field sizes

In Form or List view, you can sort database data alphanumerically.

Pull down the Record menu and click Sort Records. In the Sort Records dialog, click the arrow to the right of the Sort by field and select the field you want to sort by. Click Ascending or Descending.

If you also want to sort by subsidiary fields, complete the above procedures for either (or both) Then by fields.

Finally, click OK.

Works has a useful 'best fit' feature.

Simply click Best Fit in either dialog to have the record(s) or field(s) adjust themselves automatically to their contents.

Sooner or later, you'll find it necessary to change the dimensions of fields or records within List view. This necessity arises when there is too much data to display adequately. You can enlarge or shrink single or multiple fields/records.

Changing record height

To change one record's height, click the record number. If you want to change multiple records, hold down Shift and click the appropriate extra numbers. Then pull down the Format menu and click Record Height. Carry out the following steps:

2 Click here

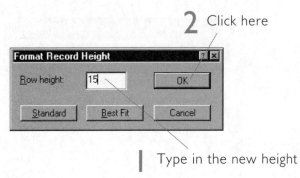

Type in the new height

Changing field widths

To change one field's width, click the field heading. If you want to change multiple fields, hold down Shift and click the appropriate extra headings. Then pull down the Format menu and click Field Width. Now do the following:

2 Click here

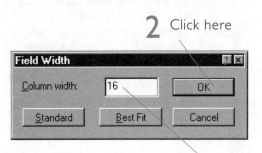

Type in the new width

Working with fills

You can 'filter' your data. Filters are criteria which determine which data is viewed. (For example, in an address book you could specify that only records whose Initials are 'S.' should display...)

To create and apply a filter, pull down the Tools menu and click Filters. In the Filter dialog, click New Filter. Name the filter, then click OK. Click the arrow to the right of the Field name box; select a field. Click the arrow to the right of the Comparison field; select a comparison type. In the Compare To field, type the text or values you want Works to match. Repeat the above for any further comparisons. Finally, click Apply Filter.

In List view, you can have the contents of a selected field entry automatically copied into other field entries or records.

Use this technique to save time and effort.

Duplicating a field entry

Click the field entry whose contents you want to duplicate. Then move the mouse pointer over the appropriate border. Click and hold down the button; drag the border over the field entries or records into which you want the contents inserted. Release the button.

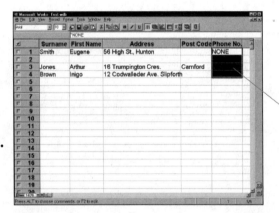

In this illustration, the contents of the Phone No. field in record I are to be copied into the same field entries in records 2-4

Now pull down the Edit menu and click Fill Right or Fill Down, as appropriate.

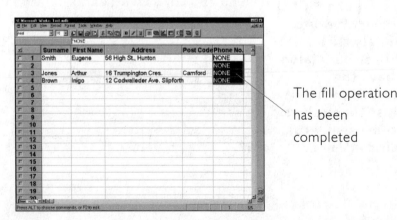

The fill operation has been completed

Working with fill series

You can spell-check database contents. Press F7. Complete the Spelling dialog in line with the procedures on page 71.

You can also carry out fills which *extrapolate* field entry contents over the specified entries. Look at the next illustration:

The start of a series

If (as here) you wanted to insert month names in successive field entries, you could do so manually. But there's a much easier way. You can have Works do it for you.

Creating a series

Type in the first element(s) of the series in consecutive field entries. Select the entries. Then pull down the Edit menu and click Fill Series. Now do the following:

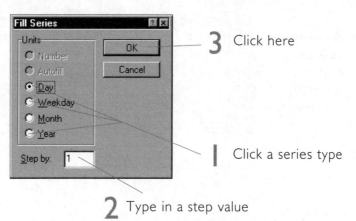

Re step 2 – the step value sets the rate by which the series progresses. Use plus numbers for increments, minus numbers for decrements.
  For example, setting -2 in this instance would produce the following series:
November, September, July, May
and so on...

3 Click here

| Click a series type

2 Type in a step value

Changing fonts and styles

HANDY TIP

You can carry out any of these from within List or Form Design views. Note, however, that the results are independent – e.g. you can colour the same field red in Form Design view and blue in List view.

The Database module lets you carry out the following actions on field contents (numbers, text or combinations of both):

- apply a new font

- apply a new type size

- apply a font style (*Italic*, **Bold**, <u>Underlining</u> or ~~Strikethrough~~)

- apply a colour

Amending the appearance of field contents

Select the data you want to reformat. Pull down the Format menu and click Font and Style. Carry out step 1 below. Now follow any of steps 2-5, as appropriate. Finally, carry out step 6.

1 │ Ensure this tab is active 3 Type in a type size

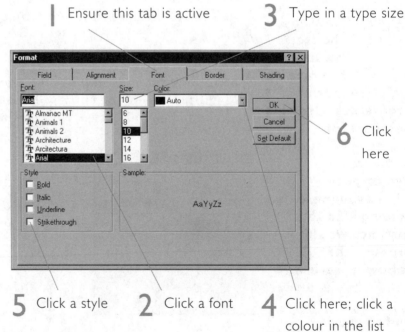

6 Click here

HANDY TIP

Re step 5 – you can apply multiple styles, if you want.

5 Click a style 2 Click a font 4 Click here; click a colour in the list

Aligning field contents

You can apply the following alignments to field entries:

REMEMBER

The full alignment options are only available within List view.

Horizontal alignment

General   the default (text to the left, numbers to the right)

Left   contents are aligned from the left

Right   contents are aligned from the right

Center   contents are centred

Vertical alignment

Top   contents align with the top of the field(s)

Center   contents are centred

Bottom   contents align with the field bottom

Customising alignment & applying text wrap

Select the relevant field(s). Pull down the Format menu and click Alignment. Carry out step 1. Now follow any or all of steps 2-4, as appropriate. Finally, carry out step 5.

REMEMBER

Re step 3 – when text wrap is selected, any surplus text within a field is forced onto separate lines within the field.
   Note that text wrap is only available within List view.

Ensure this tab is active

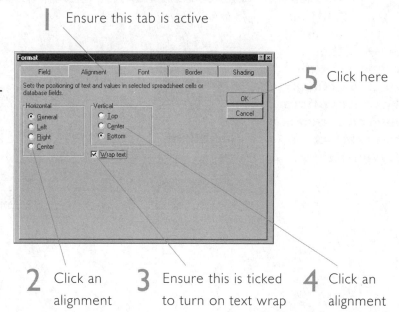

5 Click here

2 Click an alignment

3 Ensure this is ticked to turn on text wrap

4 Click an alignment

Bordering fields

HANDY TIP

You can border fields in Form Design view, too. However, you can only create *perimeter* borders.

In List view, you can define a border around:

- the perimeter of selected field(s)

- the individual fields *within* a group of selected fields

- specific field sides

You can customise the border by choosing from a selection of pre-defined border styles. You can also colour it, if required.

Applying a field border

First, click the heading(s) of the field(s) you want to border. Pull down the Format menu and click Border. Now carry out steps 1 and 2 below. Step 3 is optional. Finally, follow step 4. (If you're setting multiple border options, repeat steps 2-4 as required). Finally, carry out step 5:

HANDY TIP

Re step 4 – Outline borders the perimeter of the selected field(s). The other options (you can click more than 1) affect *individual* sides.

1 Ensure this tab is active

2 Click the relevant line style option

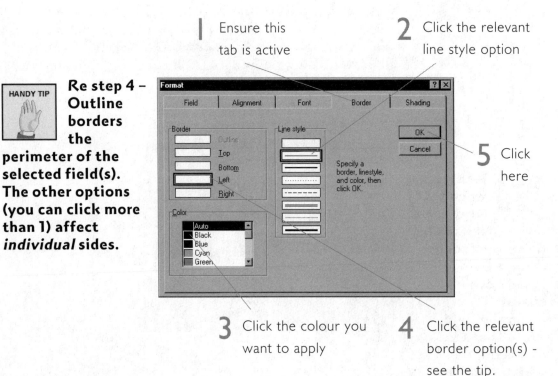

5 Click here

3 Click the colour you want to apply

4 Click the relevant border option(s) - see the tip.

Shading fields

In List view, you can apply the following to fields:

- a pattern

- a pattern colour

- a background colour

HANDY TIP

You can apply these in Form Design view, too. Note, however, that if no fields have been pre-selected they apply to the *whole* of the form.

You can do any of these singly, or in combination. Interesting effects can be achieved by using pattern colours with coloured backgrounds.

Applying a pattern or background

First, select the heading(s) of the field(s) you want to shade. Pull down the Format menu and click Shading. Now carry out step 1 below. Follow steps 2, 3 and/or 4 as appropriate. Finally, carry out step 5:

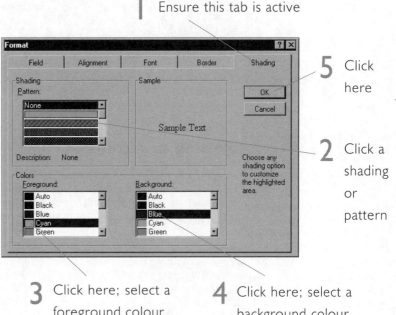

Ensure this tab is active

5 Click here

2 Click a shading or pattern

HANDY TIP

The Sample field previews how your background and pattern/colour will look.

3 Click here; select a foreground colour

4 Click here; select a background colour

Find operations

The Database module lets you search for text and/or numbers. There are two basic options. You can:

- have the first matching record display

- view all records which contain the specified text or numbers

If the Find dialog does not allow you to carry out a precise enough search, use filters instead. (See the REMEMBER tip on page 170 for how to use them).

Searching for data

Pull down the Edit menu and click Find (or press Ctrl+F). Now carry out step 1 below, then *either* step 2 or 3. Finally, carry out step 4:

Type in the data you want to find

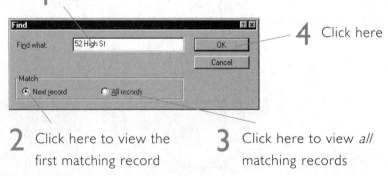

4 Click here

2 Click here to view the first matching record

3 Click here to view *all* matching records

Showing all records again

If you followed step 3 above, Works will only display matching records (other records in your database are inaccessible). To show all records again, pull down the Record menu and do the following:

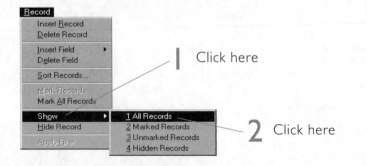

Click here

2 Click here

Search-and-replace operations

When you search for data, you can also – if you want – have Works replace it with something else.

You can specify the search direction:

Records   the search is left-to-right

Fields   the search is top-to-bottom

You can only carry out a search-and-replace operation in List view.

Running a search-and-replace operation

Pull down the Edit menu and click Replace. Now carry out step 1-3 below. Now do *one* of the following:

— Follow step 4. When Works locates the first search target, carry out step 5 to have it replaced. Repeat this process as often as necessary.

— Carry out step 6 to have Works find every target and replace it automatically.

1 Type in the data you want to find   **4** Click here to find the 1st occurrence   **5** Click here to replace it

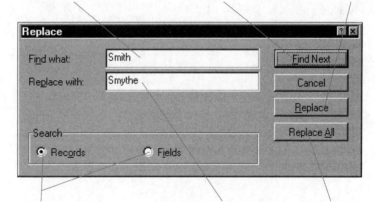

3 To specify the search direction, click the relevant option   **2** Type in the replacement data   **6** Click here to replace *all* occurrences

Page setup – an overview

When you come to print out your database, it's important to ensure the page setup is correct. Luckily, Works makes this easy.

See the HANDY TIP on page 181 for extra page setup features which are only available in Form view.

Page setup features you can customise (in List and Form view) include:

•   the paper size

•   the page orientation

•   the starting page number

•   margins

•   whether gridlines are printed

•   whether record and field headings are printed

Field headings

This is a section of a database viewed in Print Preview mode – see pages 183-185.

	Surname	First Name	Address	Post Code	Phone No.
1	Smith	Eugene	56 High St., Hunton		
2	Jones	Arthur	16 Trumping Camford		
3	Brown	Inigo	12 Codwalleder Ave. Slipforth		
4	Smith				

Record headings

Margin settings you can amend are:

—   the top margin

—   the bottom margin

—   the left margin

—   the right margin

When you save your active database, all page setup settings are saved with it.

Setting size/orientation options

Version 4 has fewer pre-defined paper types.

The Database module comes with 17 pre-defined paper types which you can apply to your databases, in either portrait (top-to-bottom) or landscape (sideways on) orientation.

Portrait orientation

Landscape orientation

If none of the supplied page definitions is suitable, you can create your own.

Applying a new page size/orientation

Pull down the File menu and click Page Setup. Now carry out step 1 below, followed by steps 2-3 as appropriate. Finally, carry out step 4:

To create your own paper size, click Custom Size in step 2. Then type in the appropriate measurements in the Height & Width fields.
   Finally, carry out steps 3-4.

1 Ensure this tab is active

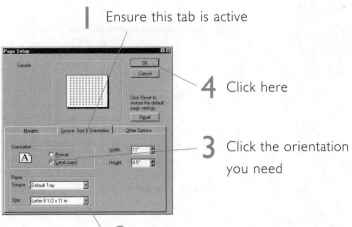

4 Click here

3 Click the orientation you need

2 Click here; click the page size you need in the drop-down list

Setting margin options

The Database module lets you set a variety of margin settings. The illustration below shows the main ones:

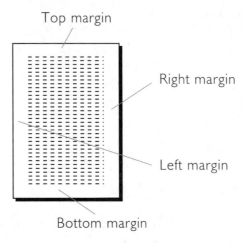

Top margin

Right margin

Left margin

Bottom margin

Applying new margins

Pull down the File menu and click Page Setup. Now carry out step 1-3 below:

1 Ensure this tab is active

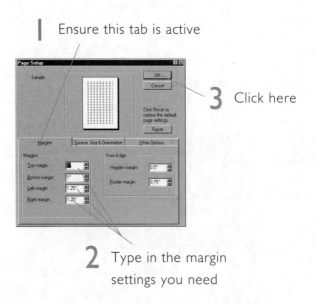

3 Click here

2 Type in the margin settings you need

Other page setup options

You can determine whether gridlines and record/field headers print. These are demonstrated below:

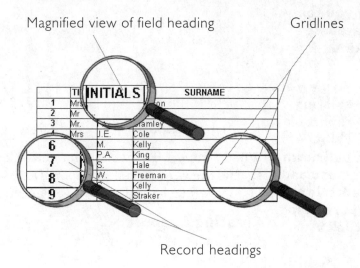

Magnified view of field heading

Gridlines

Record headings

You can also set the page number for the first page in your database – the default is: '1'.

To apply a new start number, type it into the Starting page number: field.

Printing gridlines and record/field headings

Pull down the File menu and click Page Setup. Now carry out step 1 below, followed by step 2 as appropriate. Finally, carry out step 3:

Ensure this tab is active

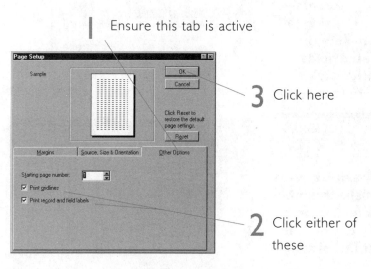

3 Click here

2 Click either of these

If you launch this dialog from within Form view, step 2 initiates lines between fields and/or page breaks between records. You can also set the inter-record gap.

Report creation

You can use a special Database feature – ReportCreator – to compile a report according to the criteria you set. When you use ReportCreator, you can specify:

- how the report is named (you can also allocate a working title/heading)

- which fields are included

- the order in which fields are arranged ('sorting')

- which records are included ('filtering')

When a report has been generated, Works stores it in a special view mode called Report Definition. This resembles List view (but has labelled rows, not numbered records).

Creating a report

Pull down the Tools menu and click ReportCreator. Do the following:

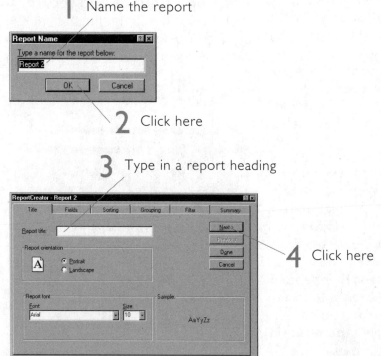

1 Name the report

2 Click here

3 Type in a report heading

4 Click here

Using Print Preview

The Database module provides a special view mode called Print Preview. This displays the active database (one page at a time) exactly as it will look when printed. Use Print Preview as a final check just before you begin printing.

When you're using Print Preview, you can zoom in or out on the active page. What you can't do, however, is:

- display more than one page at a time

- edit or revise the active document

Launching Print Preview
Pull down the File menu and click Print Preview. This is the result:

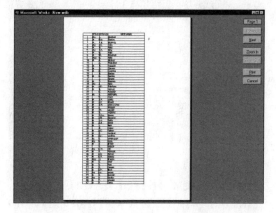

A database in
List view,
viewed in
Print Preview

**You can use a keyboard shortcut to leave Print Preview mode and return to your database.
Simply press Esc.**

A database in
Form view,
viewed in
Print Preview

Zooming in or out in Print Preview

There are two methods you can use here.

Using the mouse

Move the mouse pointer over the page area; it changes to a magnifying glass. Position this over the portion of the active database which you want to expand. Left-click once. Repeat this if necessary.

When you've reached the limit of magnification which Works supports, left-clicking with the mouse *decreases* **the magnification.**

A magnified view of part of a List view database in Print Preview

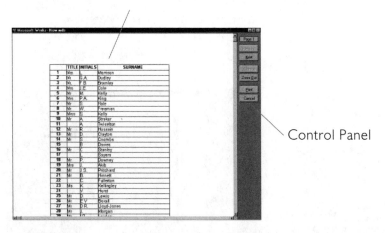

Control Panel

Using the Control Panel

Launch Print Preview. Then carry out the following actions:

Depending on the current level of magnification, one of the Zoom buttons may be greyed out, and therefore unavailable.

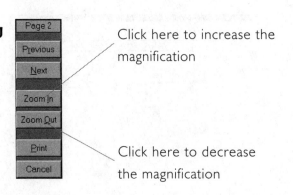

Click here to increase the magnification

Click here to decrease the magnification

Changing pages in Print Preview

Although you can only view one page at a time in Print Preview mode, you can step backwards and forwards through the database as often as necessary.

There are three methods you can use (in descending order of usefulness).

Using the Control Panel
Carry out the following actions:

 Depending on your location within the document (and the number of pages), one of these buttons may be greyed out, and therefore unavailable.

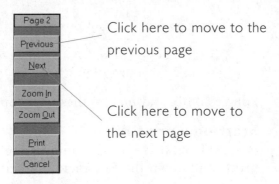

Click here to move to the previous page

Click here to move to the next page

Using the keyboard
You can use the following keyboard shortcuts:

 In a magnified page view, the Page Up and Page Down keys move through the current page.

Page Up	Moves to the previous page (unavailable within a magnified page view)
Page Down	Moves to the next page (unavailable within a magnified page view)
Up cursor	Within a magnified view of a page, moves towards the top of the page
Down cursor	Within a magnified view of a page, moves towards the base of the page

Using the scroll bars
When you're working with a magnified view of a page, use the vertical and/or horizontal scroll bars (using standard Windows techniques) to move up or down within the page.

Printing database data

When you print your data within List view, you can specify:

 If you're printing from within Form view, you have a further choice. Click Current record only to limit the print run to the active record.

- the number of copies you want printed

- whether you want the copies 'collated'. This is the process whereby Works prints one full copy at a time. For instance, if you're printing four copies of a 20-page database, Works prints pages 1-20 of the first copy, followed by pages 1-20 of the second and pages 1-20 of the third... And so on.

- which pages you want printed

- the printer you want to use (if you have more than one installed on your system)

You can 'mix and match' these, as appropriate.

Starting a print run

Open the database which contains the data you want to print. Pull down the File menu and click Print.

 If this *isn't* the first print run in your current session, simply perform steps 3-7 on page 187.

If this is the first time you've initiated a print-run in your current Works session, carry out steps 1-2 below, as appropriate, then steps 3-7 on page 187.

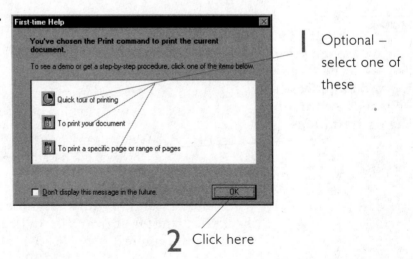

Optional – select one of these

2 Click here

...contd

To move through the tour, click either of these buttons:

 one screen back

 one screen on

To close the special tour at any time, click this button:

Done

If you followed step 1 on page 186, one of the following launches:

1. a special tour relating to printing

2. the Print dialog, plus on-screen help relating to printing

3. the Print dialog, plus help with printing page ranges

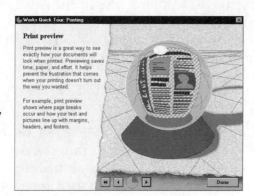

The result of 1 above

Follow steps 3-7 below, as appropriate:

If you need to adjust your printer's internal settings before you initiate printing, click Properties. Then refer to your printer's manual.

Click Draft quality printing to have your database print with minimal formatting.

3 Click here; select a printer from the list

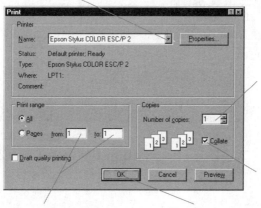

4 Type in the no. of copies required

5 Click here to turn collation on or off

6 Type a page range

7 Click here

Printing – the fast track approach

Since databases and printing needs vary dramatically, it's often necessary to customise print options before you begin printing.

For example, if you've created a complex database, you may well want to print out a draft copy for proofing purposes prior to printing the definitive version (although Print Preview mode provides a very effective indication of how a document will look when printed, there are still errors which are only detectable when you're working with hard copy). In this situation, you may wish to print in Draft mode (with minimal formatting).

For how to set your own print options, see the pages 186-187.

On the other hand, simple databases can often benefit from a simple approach. In this case, you may well be content to print using the default options. Works recognises this and provides a method which bypasses the standard Print dialog, and is therefore much quicker and easier to use.

Printing with the current print options

First, ensure your printer is ready, and your database is ready to print. Make sure the Toolbar is visible. (If it isn't, pull down the View menu and click Toolbar).

Now do the following:

Click here

Works starts printing the active database immediately.

Index